C000260531

DEAL

Guide to Buying a Second-hand Car

M   Aug   July
     1994 - 1995

N   95 - 96

P   96 - 97

R   97   98

S   98 - 99

Guide to Buying a Second-hand Car

James Ruppert

Introduction by
Mike Brewer and Richard Sutton

CHANNEL 4 BOOKS

First published in 1999 by Channel 4 Books, an imprint of
Macmillan Publishers Ltd, 25 Eccleston Place, London SW1W 9NF
and Basingstoke.

Associated companies throughout the world.

ISBN 0 7522 1771 2

Text © James Ruppert, 1999

Introduction © Mike Brewer and Richard Sutton, 1999

The right of James Ruppert to be identified as the author of this work has
been asserted by him in accordance with the Copyright, Designs and Patents
Act 1988.

All rights reserved. No part of this publication may be reproduced, stored in or
introduced into a retrieval system, or transmitted, in any form, or by any
means (electronic, mechanical, photocopying, recording or otherwise) without
the prior written permission of the publisher. Any person who does any
unauthorized act in relation to this publication may be liable to criminal
prosecution and civil claims for damage.

1 3 5 7 9 8 6 4 2

A CIP catalogue record for this book is
available from the British Library.

Design by Ben Cracknell Studios

All photographs courtesy of James Ruppert and all manufacturers
except page 66 © BMIHT/Rover Group

Black-and-white reproduction by Speedscan Ltd

Printed in England by Bath Press Ltd

This book is sold subject to the condition that it shall not, by way of trade or
otherwise, be lent, resold, hired out, or otherwise circulated without the
publisher's prior consent in any form of binding or cover other than that in
which it is published and without a similar condition including this condition
being imposed on the subsequent purchaser.

This book accompanies the television series *Deals on Wheels*
made by Ideal World for Channel 4.

Executive producer: Zad Rogers

Contents

Introduction 6
by Mike Brewer and Richard Sutton

Introduction

There can be little doubt that one of the most traumatic financial issues that most of us have to face is the buying and selling of our trusty friends and servants – our cars. Buying a car can be a stressful business and, with many of us changing our cars on average every two or three years, the process is almost inescapable for every private motorist.

A car is likely to be the second most expensive purchase you make after your house. The fact is an ordinary person can have a significant chunk of their annual income wiped out by buying a dud car so it pays to be armed with as much information as possible. This is why we created *Deals on Wheels*, Channel 4's weekly guide to the rights and wrongs of buying and selling used cars.

No doubt you have earned every penny of the money you will spend on your next car. Perhaps you have saved for ages, looked forward to the big purchase day for weeks, or will have to pay off a loan for years. Yet, for the sake of taking the right advice, you could lose a fortune by paying too much or selling too cheap.

Time and again at *Deals on Wheels* we hear stories of the proverbial little old lady who has let her three-year-old Fiesta go for the value of a five-year-old one. Why? Because she thought that the 'terribly nice young man' who came to buy it was telling her the truth. And time and again we hear of people simply offering to pay the asking price because they felt it was a good price. Perhaps it was, but you can almost guarantee that they would have saved a small fortune had they had the presence of mind to haggle properly. Not haggling at the point of purchase is just plain daft, no matter how fair you think the asking price is.

The fact remains that when buying and selling your car you have to adopt a trader's frame of mind, otherwise, sure as day, you will lose money and probably a great deal. *Deals on Wheels* aims to show, by example, what really goes on.

Deals on Wheels: Guide to Buying a Second-hand Car is designed as an aid to doing a good deal. It is written in an easy-to-understand way that will help you avoid the usual pitfalls. It will help you choose the best car for you, while steering you through the inevitable perils that threaten every potential purchase. In this business the early bird catches the worm and it pays to be as well versed as possible. So on the day, having read this book, you should have an idea of the type of car you want and your budget.

James Ruppert's book guides you through the whole process from the decision to look for a car to the deal itself. If you are selling it will help you advertise effectively, treat the strangers coming to see the car appropriately, get the price you want and generally reduce those dreadful stomach butterflies every seller knows so well. As a buyer it will enable you to reassure the seller that you are well informed and knowledgeable and so help you to direct the negotiations in the way you want them to go. *Deals on Wheels: Guide to Buying a Second-hand Car* also includes useful information specific to the top fifty most popular cars on the market together with our special *Deals on Wheels* rating for each.

After reading this book we hope you will feel confident enough to go out and get your car at the price you can afford and so ensure that your next motor deal is a treat rather than a tragedy.

We hope you get the deal you're looking for.

Good luck!

Mike Brewer and Richard Sutton

Before You Buy

Before you go anywhere near a used car you must get a few things straight – like where is the money coming from? What sort of car do I really need? Can I get insurance? What about my old car? Only when those questions have been answered can you start planning where to look for your used car.

Money Matters

Budget

Simple question: how much can you actually afford? That is your budget. We'd all love to spend £50,000 on our next car, but you must be realistic. Add up all your weekly/monthly outgoings and expenditures and set that against your income. Obvious really. What's left is how much you have to cover insurance, road tax insurance, fuel costs and maintenance of your next car. Is it enough? Do you have savings? Are you prepared to spend all or some of that on buying the car? By the end of this chapter you will have worked out these costs, but for now set yourself a buying budget and stick to it. Haven't got the savings? Then ...

Borrowing

The simplest is the loan, where the amount borrowed is paid back, plus interest over an agreed period to the lender. Available from a bank, building society, credit card company and some finance companies. It can be secured, so you offer something as security in return for the money borrowed, usually your home. The rate of interest may be variable; it will be cheaper than an unsecured loan, the amount borrowed higher and the repayment period longer. An unsecured Loan is not backed by any security and the rate of interest is usually fixed. As there is lots of competition, interest rates can vary considerably. If the lender accepts your application, you will sign an agreement and the money can be paid into your bank, or building society account, or to you as a cheque, or banker's draft in the name of the dealer.

Car dealer's credit

There are many different consumer credit options. A conditional sale is the normal way that a car dealer operates. The customer pays a deposit, followed by the balance with interest, by fixed instalments over a contract period. The vehicle is sold to the customer, provided that all the payments are made and the car is comprehensively insured and maintained in good condition. Ownership of the car passes when the last payment is made. With hire purchase the terms are similar, but the customer effectively hires the car with a final option to pay a lump sum and actually buy the car at the end of the contract period. Personal leasing is similar to hiring in that the customer never owns the vehicle and typically at the end of the contract period replaces the car with another. Personal Contract Purchase (PCP) schemes are essentially new car-buying packages similar to a personal lease.

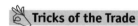 **Tricks of the Trade**

- The problem with PCP and lease schemes is that it leaves the buyer without any equity and the only way out is to sign up for another PCP or similar buying package from the same company.

- Some dealers who offer loans for any deposit get high commission for these sums and the interest rate may also be unfavourable.

Deciding on the best scheme

In order to decide on the best way forward you must ask yourself whether you want to own the car at the end of the period. Then calculate what you will actually be paying for the car, including the interest over the loan period.

Anyone with a little money for a deposit ought to consider a personal contract hire scheme, which is effectively a hire agreement, at the end of which period the car is handed back to the dealer. There will be mileage restrictions and it could suit someone who has been used to running a company car. If you can afford a substantial deposit then a hire purchase scheme is worth considering, as the monthly payments are lower and you can own the car at the end of the period.

Which lender?

Always read the terms and conditions of the scheme and shop around for the best deal for you. First, you need to consider the Annual Percentage Rate (APR) which lenders must quote by law; the lower it is, the cheaper it will be to borrow money from them. Banks may negotiate a lower rate of interest, whereas building societies usually offer the lowest interest rates of all. Remember also to compare any finance arrangement fees and penalties that could be imposed for exceeding a mileage limit, or for settling the loan early. What you need to calculate is the total cost of borrowing the money. This can be done by comparing what the cost of the car would have been outright and what you will have paid overall at the end of the finance agreement.

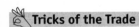 **Tricks of the Trade**

- If a finance company requires a larger deposit, or guarantor, some dealers may use this as an excuse to raise the interest rate.
- The repayment period, for example, £200 a month over three years is £1200 more than two years at £250 a month.
- Quoting weekly payments is a way of making large sums seem smaller and easier to pay.
- Don't give a dealer all your personal details before deciding to buy. They may use them to get quotes for the best commission rates and that may show up as a large number of bad finance searches against your name.

Which Car?

The basics

You would think that deciding what type of car you want would be easy. Not so. Lots of people leave their house having decided on a three-door hatchback, only to leave the showroom a few hours later in a stretch limousine. Salesmen can be very persuasive and it is all too easy to fall in love with something inappropriate and impractical. You must decide on a type, or range, of car and stick to it. Our Deals On Wheels Top Fifty (see pages 31–131) will undoubtedly help with the finer details, but before you start comparing models you should get the basics of what you need sorted out.

Size matters

How big is your drive, garage, carport, or even parking space outside your house, or place of work? There is no point buying a car that is going to be too big. Take measurements. Don't forget that it isn't just you who will be using the car. Dogs and children must also be able to fit in. Bad back, tall, short, fat, thin: we are all different shapes and have different ailments. If you want to avoid the osteopath's table, make sure the driver's seat is supportive, the steering column adjusts and you can see out clearly. What do you want your next car to do? Tow a caravan? Then it needs a large engine and maybe four-wheel drive. For local journeys, a small hatchback will do. If you have hobbies to follow up at weekends maybe an estate would be good. Only you know. There is nothing worse than having the wrong car for the job. An off-roader just for the urban school run is stupid, but so is a cramped coupé for a family of four. Think hard before you buy.

Petrol versus Diesel

The case for buying a used diesel car seems to be getting weaker all the time, even though some arguments in favour are strong:

For
- Fuel economy is very high.
- Engines are mechanically simple.
- That makes them more reliable.
- Ideal then, if you are thinking of becoming a taxi driver.

Against
- They are worked hard, habitually run up huge hundred-thousand mileages, then get sold off, often with the mileage readjusted and requiring a major engine overhaul.
- Sellers think they are worth more – not necessarily.
- Need more frequent oil changes and servicing than petrol vehicles.
- Diesel is environmentally unfriendly; there are toxic particles in the exhaust which can cause cancer and asthma.
- Slow, especially non-turbo versions.
- Fuel is smelly, slippery and difficult to get off clothes and hands; not a nice experience at the pumps.
- Nor is it significantly cheaper than petrol, unlike in Europe.

Buy a diesel
- If a catalytic converter is fitted to clean up the exhaust.
- Only if you do a huge annual mileage.
- If you can afford a top of the range BMW, or equivalent, which has a state of the art turbo-diesel unit which is difficult to distinguish from a petrol one.

Diesel can be a false economy and suits only a minority of drivers. Potentially a bad used buy.

Image is everything

Even though we like to think we'd only buy a car for sensible, practical and financial reasons, actually what the car looks like, and says about us, is often a vitally important part of the decision-making process. It is all about credibility and some cars have it, while others don't. A strong image means a car will hold its value well and be easier to resell. For example a VW Golf has a fine reputation for reliability and economy, but is also well styled and very highly regarded as subtle, classless transportation with a large youth following. By contrast the identical (except for a big rear boot) VW Vento/Jetta looks ugly and is unpopular, yet is just as well built and reliable. High-image makes include BMW, Mercedes, Audi, as are small Renaults, Peugeots, Citroens and Fiats. Low-image makes include Skodas, Hyundais, Protons, big Renaults, Citroens and Peugeots. To find out about image look at what fashionable people are driving. Read style magazines and also car magazines to find out what's hip and what isn't. The bottom line is, if you don't care about image, or future resale value, you stand a very good chance of picking up a cheap car. The choice is yours.

Extra, extra

What a used car comes fitted with is extremely important. It won't necessarily make it worth more, but it will be easier to live with and eventually resell. The number of really important extras is small. Safety sells, so ABS brakes and air bags are good news. Big luxury/executive cars must have leather trim and automatic gearboxes. Small cars don't need much, although power steering is nice. Don't pay more for an expensive music system, alloy wheels, or anything else which is 'tarting up' an otherwise ordinary car, like a cheap bodykit and spoilers. Non-manufacturer-fitted engine immobilisers and alarms can go wrong. Colour matters. White, especially on larger cars, is awful. Anything dull, such as brown, is bad. Flat colours must be strong. Metallics are best, but again they must be strong. Fashionable colours, like bright yellow, have a habit of going out of fashion, so choose carefully, or pay a lot less. The golden rule is, buy the best-equipped car you can afford, but never pay extra for extras.

Insurance Matters

So you have sort of decided what model and maybe what make of car you'd like to buy. How about insurance then? Ignore this important matter until the last minute and it could be something that a car dealer will be happy to organise, at a price! Sorting it out now is the sensible thing to do, because it could help you change your mind about the sort of car you intend to look for.

Shopping for insurance is easy, you just have to invest a bit of time on the phone – on the plus side, many numbers will be freephone ones. Best of all, the insurance industry has never been more competitive.

Decide on the cover you want

Third party, fire and theft covers the damage you do to someone else, and their property, also allowing for the car to be stolen, or set alight. This is worth considering for an old and very cheap car. Then there is comprehensive cover, which pays for most of the damage resulting from an accident – much better for a more valuable car and for peace of mind as hire-car charges and tow-in fees could be covered.

Factors affecting insurance

The car Ease of repair, cost of repair, performance, cost when new. Also any modifications may affect the amount the policy costs, i.e. tuning the engine, or fitting alloy wheels. Fitting extra security measures, though, should help reduce the premium.

Your home The more densely populated the area, the higher the chances of theft or an accident. Garaging a car often helps reduce the premium.

Use Lots of named drivers raises the price of a premium; also if the car is used primarily for business rather than social, domestic and pleasure purposes.

You A bad risk because of your driving record? Anyone under twenty-five years old automatically pays a higher premium. Over fifty? Good news – you are less of a risk and should pay less.

Policy details

Excess A voluntary and also compulsory amount; an agreed sum that you will pay in the event of a claim, e.g. the first £100. The higher the excess then the lower the premium.

No claims discount Building up a claims-free driving record means the cost of the policy will be reduced each year, until the discount reaches 60 per cent. This bonus can also be protected for an extra amount, in the event of having to make a claim.

Special policies These are available for certain kinds of drivers in particular professions (e.g. hairdressers), or people over a certain age (mature drivers). Women are also considered a better risk and some insurance companies will offer lower premiums. Under this category also come classic-car policies (mostly for cars over twenty years old), where account is taken of how cherished the car is, and the mileage is likely to be restricted annually (e.g. around five thousand miles).

Brokers versus direct insurers

Contact both. Brokers operate between insurance firms and you, the policyholder. They are not necessarily more expensive than a direct insurer, and can be much more flexible in placing a special risk, or simply finding the right insurance company for you. Direct insurers are competitive and can often specialise in certain kinds of customer, e.g. mature drivers. Get at least ten quotes based on exactly the same requirements and then compare the cover and additional benefits on offer, these may include free windscreen replacement, or even membership of a rescue organisation.

Sell Your Old Car

If you have one, don't forget about your old car; it's worth something, and here's how you should go about selling it.

Be prepared

Clean the car. This sounds really obvious, but it is surprising how many sellers forget. Any buyer, whether private or trade, is more likely to buy a tidy, clean and attractive car. Skips on wheels don't sell. Even an old banger responds well to a wash and vacuum. If you can't be bothered, or your car is in pretty good condition anyway, consider a professional valet. For a relatively small sum almost any car will look like new again.

Find every scrap of paper you have relating to the car. Obviously the most recent MOT certificate and the V5 registration document are the most important, but also all bills, warranties and service records. Put these in a ring-binder folder. It proves to the potential buyer that you have cared for the car and they can easily and conveniently see the car's history. Like the car being presented clean, first impressions count.

Look at the prices similar cars to yours are selling for locally, which is probably the best way of arriving at a figure. Also buy car valuation guides, like *Parker's*, from the newsagent which will help you set a figure. Remember to allow yourself a small margin for negotiation of around ten per cent.

Advertise

First, pick your market. A cheap car should only be advertised locally, so the newspaper, free sheet, *Loot*, or bargain section of the *Auto Trader* publication will all do. A more valuable current model could equally do well in the relevant part of those publications, but also in *Exchange & Mart*. If you have something, which is a classic, then try a classic-car magazine. Expensive cars need expensive advertising solutions, such as the *Sunday Times*.

What you must mention in order to sell your car is the year and registration letter, e.g. 1987 D, or E? Buyers know the difference. Give the service history, if any, mileage if known and owners if very few. Identify the engine size, whether it is a diesel, turbo, automatic and whether a GL or GLX. Mention less obvious luxuries such as a CD player. Buyers like to know the colour and also mention if it's metallic. Be specific about price, never say 'offers'. And don't forget your telephone number.

When people call in response, be polite and positive, give as much information as possible, don't lie, or make promises that can't be kept about the condition of the car. Don't negotiate the price and don't make an appointment to view until you have taken down their number and rung them back. The appointment to view must be at a convenient time for you. Make sure that you are not alone when the buyer, or buyers, call. Tell buyers to bring their driving licence and proof that their insurance covers this.

Buyer Arrives

Be friendly, helpful, show them the car, make sure it is open and then leave them to it, but stay in the vicinity. Go and prod at the garden, so that when they want to know something, or to go for a drive, you're on hand. It is better for you to be cool rather than desperate. Treat every potential buyer with caution. Ninety-nine per cent are genuine, but some are looking to acquire a car for nothing, by theft or fraud.

If you don't like the buyer for any reason, or feel suspicious, then refuse a test drive politely. Otherwise inspect their driving licence, note down details and check that the same name appears on the insurance certificate. Only you and, if necessary, your friend go out with the buyer. Never be outnumbered in the car. You drive first to show how smoothly it can be driven. When it is the buyer's turn to drive, take the ignition keys out and don't give them to the driver until you are back in the car.

The Deal

After the test drive is a good time to ask the buyer if they want to buy. Decide how much you would accept for the car and stick to it. Don't babble on about selling the car. State your final price and shut up.

If you make a sale, write a simple contract including details of the car, names of both parties, price, deposit paid and most importantly 'Sold as seen'. Give this to the buyer.

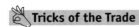 **Tricks of the Trade**

If the phone keeps ringing, keep on taking potential buyers' details. Until the buyer pays in full, it is not their car and the deal could still fall through.

And finally, don't hand over the car until you have been paid, ideally in cash. Cheques must be cleared. Building society cheques and banker's drafts can be forged. You have been warned.

Alternatively ...

You could sell the car direct to a car dealer, or trader. The disadvantage is that they will only pay the trade value for the car. The newsagent-purchased price guide like *Parker's* will tell you how much this is. It can be a lot less hassle, though, and you get cash straight away. Otherwise, you could simply part-exchange the car (see Finding a Car pages 18–22).

Finding a Car

The final piece in the buying jigsaw is deciding exactly where to look. There have never been more options for the used car buyer; whether you just want to thumb through local newspapers, tramp the streets, or even surf the Internet. There are plenty of pros and cons when it comes to taking any of these routes. Here is the DOW no-nonsense guide to shopping for a good used car.

Buying Privately

It can go either way. You could come across a decent, honest and helpful private seller with a perfect specimen to sell, or you could meet a rogue with a rough old car. You never can tell. The majority of private sellers are honest, but may have bought an awful car without realising it. Maybe they have lost all the service history; possibly their advertisement misdescribes the car. Worst of all, they think their car is worth a fortune. So if you think buying from the motor trade is fraught with danger, DOW suggests that you need to be very switched on when buying a car privately.

You have fewer legal rights if you buy privately. The car must be as described by the seller. If a private seller lies about the condition of the car, you can sue for your losses, provided you can find the seller again and want to go to the trouble of pursuing a claim through the civil courts.

There is a huge amount of difference between a private seller against whom a buyer has virtually no redress, and a full-time dealer who has all sorts of legal obligations to verify mileage and describe the car accurately. Trying to find out whether you have found a closet trader is common sense, and give-aways will include a slick manner, unconvincing reasons for selling, more than one car for sale when you call and mobile-telephone contact numbers. Maybe the seller wants to meet somewhere other than at their home. Maybe you can only phone them at a specific time, because they are using a public phone.

Buying from a Dealer

Buying from a dealer is not as risky as it used to be. There is a lot of consumer protection, especially if you deal with a large, or long-established company. If you want to buy what are arguably the best cars and choose from the largest stock in your area, then your local franchised dealers will probably have them, but at a price. Remember that you will be paying for all those potted plants and floor tiles, by paying top money for their used cars. In that case, you can expect and demand the best, and with that comes the best protection. In most cases this will mean a comprehensive manufacturer-backed warranty, such as that operated by Ford and their Direct scheme, or Vauxhall's Network Q, both of which are excellent. All dealers, though, offer some form of mechanical breakdown insurance posing as a guarantee, although the terms and conditions have to be read very carefully, as there can be lots of exclusions.

Legally a car sold by a dealer must be of satisfactory quality, or of a standard that a reasonable person would regard as acceptable, bearing in mind the way it was described, how much it cost and any other relevant circumstances. This covers, for example, the appearance and finish of the car, its safety and its durability. It must be free from defects, except when they were pointed out to you by the dealer, and as described – a one-owner car must be just that. It must also be fit for any normal purpose – so it must be a reasonably reliable car and capable of any tasks you specify, like seating seven passengers, or towing a caravan.

Classified advertisements placed by a dealer or car trader must have a T at the end of them.

Other Possibilities

Brokers

Although strongly associated with the new-car market, independent brokers can also source nearly-new, ex-management and ex-dealer demonstrator stock at significant savings. They advertise in car magazines and newspapers. It is worth asking lots of questions: some cars could be those returned under a 'no-quibble new car warranty scheme', and could be faulty. Beware any brokers who ask for a big deposit and establish where the car is coming from before handing over any money.

For: They do the haggling for you.

Against: But some may string you along without having access to the car you really want to buy.

Car supermarkets

More new cars than the market knew what to do with has resulted in the overspill being stocked at so-called car supermarkets, where hundreds of cars can be found on sale. Their philosophy of 'park them deep and sell them cheap' has largely worked, although it is not always possible to haggle a better deal. Also, their part-exchange offers can sometimes be disappointing. Car supermarkets are best for nearly new cars, as older stock direct from auctions can look shabby and poor value. As ever, the golden rule is shop around.

For: Huge choice. Low prices.

Against: Poor part-exchange deals.

The Internet

One of the newest and most remarkable car-buying phenomena is the Internet. From the comfort of your own computer terminal, it is possible to surf the world wide web, or, in reality, the nationwide web for a used car. So simply sit back and click your mouse. There are online editions of *Auto Trader* and *Exchange & Mart* offering excellent search facilities: by make, model, postcode and budget. This takes the strain out of reading every page of their paper editions in search of the cars you are interested in. Colour pictures are often available.

There are also dedicated Internet services, like the Virtual Showroom. Not only that; many independent and franchised dealers now have sites so that you can look at all their used stock on screen, and many manufacturers such as BMW and Vauxhall offer direct links from their sites to their dealers, who operate official used-car schemes.

For: Instantaneous. Mostly up to date.

Against: Local call costs. You can't test-drive on the Internet.

Auctions

Things happen fast at an auction – remember that and you won't go far wrong. If you miss bidding for one car, another one will be along literally in a minute. It pays to be cautious and do plenty of homework. That means several visits without your wallet to see how it all operates. Listening carefully to what the auctioneer says before each lot is vital. A one-owner example with a warranted mileage and full service history is obviously the sort to bid for. For the less experienced, it is easy to get caught out because an auction can be a clearing house for unwanted part exchanges and 'problem' cars. It is also easy to get carried away and bid too much. You will not be able to drive the car before sale, although with a warranted car the right of rejection exists for a major fault discovered within an hour after the sale.

For: Trade prices.

Against: Risky.

Making Enquiries

Most of us will respond to advertisements by telephone. That's a good idea; you don't want a wasted journey. So here are the 'must ask' questions to help you decide whether the car is worth a look.

Repeat the advert Yes, really, you must confirm that the details are correct and there are no printing errors.

Mileage? Clarify precise miles, as some ads just say 'average'.

Service records? You need to know if the miles can be backed up by real evidence.

First registered? When the car was built, which helps confirm which model it is.

MOT expiry? Some ads say 'long', or 'short' MOT.

Can the car be examined by an engineer? If the seller is reluctant, they can't be confident about their car.

Any warranties/guarantees? The seller might have an existing guarantee for a replacement engine, battery, etc.

Car tax expiry? Also, is it included in the price? Most sellers, including the trade, cash in the tax unless they agree otherwise.

Owned the car long? If a private seller has only had it a few weeks, maybe there is something wrong.

What's wrong with it? Be specific; ask about the engine, bodywork, interior.

Modified? A tuned engine or spoilers could change your opinion of the car, not to mention the insurance quote.

Previous owners? The fewer the better, obviously.

Where did you buy it? Private sellers should be able to say where it came from; family member, dealer, etc.

Registration documents? A private seller should at least have a receipt. If there's no paperwork, be suspicious, or don't bother.

Is the car on finance? If so, the finance has to be paid off before you buy.

Why selling? A private seller must have a quick and convincing answer.

Can I test-drive the car? No point turning up if you can't do this.

Do think carefully about the answers given and decide whether or not the car is worth following up. You don't have to agree right away, you can always ring the seller back. Don't agree to meet the seller halfway at a motorway service area. Maybe the car isn't theirs to sell. Also, make a daylight appointment to view.

Buying a Classic Car – A Special Case

If you have decided to buy an older classic car, often the decision has a lot to do with emotional, rather than practical reasons, but you can still go about finding and buying one in a professional, no-nonsense manner. You must find out everything you can about the classic you want. Be aware of all its faults. Drive an example (borrow or hire) to find out if you really could live with your dream classic. Join the relevant owners' club, which gives fantastic access to the best, but not necessarily the cheapest, vehicles and also lots of expert knowledge. Never buy a restoration project. It may start out cheap, but it will prove expensive and you may never finish it. Always get an expert to check the model over. That way you won't buy a dud, or pay over the odds.

Checking the Car

Anyone, without any specialist mechanical knowledge, can check out a used car and then decide whether it is worth paying for a professional second opinion.

Always look at the car in clear, dry conditions and wear old clothes. Take a copy of this book and a pen and paper. Most important of all, take a friend. They can stop you making a mistake and will be a useful extra pair of eyes and ears. Never look at a car in the rain, in the dark, or where access to it is restricted. Never allow yourself to be rushed.

Paperwork

Never overlook the bits of paper that come with a used car. Don't be distracted by shiny paintwork, or a loud stereo – ask to see the paperwork and start reading.

Service history

What you want to see is a file full of history rather than some apologetic slips of paper or just a stamped-up service book which could be forged anyway. Look at the service intervals: did the same garage do all the work? Is there a phone number of the garage to ring? Do the stamps look as though they were done at the same time? If so, this could be a forgery. Look through all the bills and make sure they are for the same vehicle; usually registration numbers are mentioned. One bill might say the car has been completely rebuilt – read everything.

MOTs

One way of confirming that the mileage is correct is to look through a succession of MOT slips and read the mileage, cross-checking it with the reading in the car. Genuine MOTs have watermarks and no alterations.

V5

Ask to see the vehicle registration document, known as the V5. If the seller does not have it, be suspicious; it means that you cannot check the car's ownership and identity details. Look at the V5 closely. Are there any spelling mistakes or alterations? If so, it may be a forgery. Hold the V5 up to the light as legitimate V5s have watermarks. If it's a private sale, ask for proof of the seller's identity and address, such as a driving licence, passport, or electricity bill. Check that the same name and address is given on the V5. Make a note of the previous owner's address – you might need it.

Check the V5 against the car – so look at the vehicle registration mark (the number plate) the vehicle identification number (VIN) – this can be found on a metal plate in the engine compartment, usually where the bonnet closes at the front, and stamped into the bodywork under the bonnet and under the driver's seat. Some cars also have the VIN etched on their windows, lamps, or mounted behind the windscreen at the passenger side of the dashboard. The engine number will be stamped on a prominent part of the engine. These numbers on the car should be the same as those on the V5. Even if they match, have the numbers been tampered with? Areas of glass may have been scratched off the windows, or stickers may cover up etching which has been altered. This is done to hide the identity of a stolen car. If in doubt, ask the seller for their insurance documents. If the car is stolen it is unlikely that they will have any, although even these documents can be forged.

Exterior

Start at the front and look along the sides of the car. Are any panels wobbly? Are they misaligned? Do they look the same from each corner of the car, front and rear? If the car does not look straight, it has been poorly repaired. Are there stone chips at the front? These are normal if the car has racked up a 70,000+ mileage, but has it? Still standing back, compare paint matches between panels. If they are different shades, then once again, could this have been in an accident and then repaired? Finally, does it sit evenly on the road? Is there a flat tyre, or is the suspension sagging because it is worn out?

Get closer. Look across the roof. The panel should be even with no signs of rough paintwork. Cars that have had major smashes often need a twisted roof to be disguised. Paintwork – does it look like an original, probably a slightly dull factory finish? Drips, an orange-peel effect, lots of blemishes and pockmarks – all indicate a respray. Look for more signs around window rubbers and under wheel arches. Excess paint gets on these areas when the car has been quickly resprayed. So why was it done? Panel gaps – are they even? Look at doors, bonnet and boot; odd gaps mean they have been bolted back on after a crash. Open the boot, lift carpets and take everything out, including the spare wheel, and look for crude repairs and fresh paint for signs of a crash. Open the bonnet – check for fresh paint, new panels, any uneven panels, or signs that a repair has taken place.

Look at the tyre tread; any uneven wear suggests that the steering is not adjusted properly, or that perhaps the wheels have been repeatedly thumped by a driver parking carelessly. Chips and scrapes on plastic wheel trims or alloy wheels will confirm this. It is also nice to see the same make and tread of tyre on each wheel, or at least matched pairs on front and rear, which shows that the previous owner cared.

Interior

Make sure that everything works. It sounds obvious, but it will pay to be very methodical about this. Sit in the driver's seat and press every knob and twist every switch. From the windscreen wipers to the electric windows, it is essential to try every gadget. Air-conditioning? Does a chilly air blow through the vents, then? Rear electric windows? Try them – most people forget.

Is the ashtray full? If the car has been professionally cleaned, but you don't fancy an ex-smoker's car, look at the roof lining for nicotine stains. There may also be cigarette burns on the seats.

Seat covers are fitted for a reason, usually to hide damage, or serious wear. Take them off and see what lurks underneath. The boot area will show signs of wear and tear certainly, but it should not look like a builder's van. If it does, avoid it; the rest of the car may not have been treated so gently either. Look at the trim and upholstery. Does it look fresh, or rather worn? What you have to decide is whether the car looks like it has covered as many miles as the seller says it has. You may have heard of 'clocking', which is altering the mileage so that the car is worth more. Even if the paperwork seems conclusive, the interior could tell a different story, so make sure that you check everything thoroughly for any tell-tale signs.

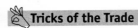

Make sure you look at the keys. Is there just the normal one, or two, to get in and start, or is there a fob full of them? Ask why the locks have been changed. The car could have been stolen, or broken into.

Spot a high-miler

Tug on the driver's seatbelt and then let go. If it snaps back, fine; if it takes forever to retract, the car has done a big mileage. Squashy, frayed and worn driver's seat? More signs that there have been lots of bums on seats. A worn and shiny steering wheel, a worn gearknob, where the H pattern is fading, worn pedal rubbers and also a hole in the driver's side carpet are all signs that the car has done at least 100,000 miles. Look at the dashboard. Are screws holding it in place worn or scratched? Does the steering wheel look out of alignment? If so, someone may have been trying to get at the mileometer to adjust the mileage. Look at the mileage reading, often when it has been tampered with the numbers are not even. If the mileage is a digital read-out, it is impossible to tell if it has been altered by a rogue with a laptop computer. The only confirmation of the true mileage is the paperwork. Is there an exclusion clause stuck over the speedometer? Then it has probably been altered. When in doubt, contact the previous owner whose address is on the V5 registration document and ask for the mileage when they sold it.

Under the Bonnet

With the engine cold. Pull out the dipstick, that is a metal stick with a round loop at the top, sited in the middle of the engine. Look at the oil. If it is black, dirty, or burnt, then it has not been serviced properly. If the level is low, then the car is either using lots of oil, or someone is not maintaining it very well. Now look at the oil filler cap located at the top of the engine. It should be clean. Any black treacle or white sludge means that not much has been done in the way of servicing. Next open the radiator cap, situated normally to one side of the engine on top of a white plastic bottle (not to be confused with the washer fluid, which is normally a larger bottle). If the water is brown, no antifreeze has been added and the water has seldom been changed. Watch out for white deposits too, which suggest a problem. Look underneath the engine; are there any oil, or water leaks? Get your friend to start the engine. A light metallic tinkle is fine, but a worn engine will crash, bang, click and clatter. Now walk around to the exhaust and ask your friend to rev hard, then back off suddenly. Lots of blue smoke, rather than a light haze, means serious engine wear.

Driving the Car

Remember to make sure that the car has a current MOT, and that you are insured to drive it. Remember to turn the radio off so you can hear what is happening. Make sure you go for a proper drive, no less than half an hour, but preferably an hour. You won't learn anything from a quick drive around the block. Try to experience as many road conditions as possible, from town to motorway.

Switch on the ignition. All the warning lights should come on (oil, ignition, brakes, etc.); if not, maybe the seller has disconnected some? Once the engine is started, all the lights should go out immediately, otherwise the engine is very worn. Also, if the engine takes an age to start, the battery, or the expensive starter motor could be on the way out. Any rough running could mean more problems to do with tuning, or maybe a very worn engine.

Power steering? While stationary, turn the wheel from lock to lock. If there are lots of squeals and strange judders, then maybe the system is very worn and it will be an expensive fix.

With a manual gearbox, is getting into gear a problem? Lots of noise, lots of free play in the lever and grinding all indicate a worn and well-used gearbox. Also, with the gears in neutral, press down the clutch pedal and listen. Any whirring noises also suggest serious wear. As for the clutch, put the handbrake on and engage first; if the car does not stall and there is a nasty smell, it may need replacing.

With an automatic gearbox the changes should be smooth and without delay and relatively silent. Applying the brake, you should be able to engage drive and reverse, then accelerate without the gearbox slipping. Otherwise, an expensive replacement or overhaul may be needed.

Try the brakes as you pull away. If they sound as though they are dragging, maybe the car has been standing for a long while and the brakes may be seized. Also, lightly touch the brakes, and if you hear an intermittent rubbing, it suggests brake disc damage. Cars fitted with ABS brakes have a warning light, which should go off soon after the car is started. If not, there could be a problem.

Checking the Car

If there is any juddering as you drive along, or if, on a quiet, flat road when you release the grip on the wheel it pulls to one side, then maybe there could be a simple cure, like a cheap wheel-balance by a local garage. Alternatively, it could mean that the car has been involved in an accident and the suspension is bent. When you turn around corners, or turn from lock to lock on the move, is there a clicking sound? If so, there is lots of wear and it will fail an MOT.

Drive over lots of rough tarmac and listen out for clonks, bangs and watch out for too many bounces. The suspension may be tired and in need of an overhaul. If you can, ride in the back of the car for a bit and listen carefully for noises there too.

Keep checking for flickering warning lights. The temperature gauge should settle in the middle of the dial. If it never moves from cold, then it has been disconnected, or if it hovers in the hot region and you can hear a fan cutting in, it's about to overheat. Ticking sounds can come from the speedometer; make sure too that it is working.

Look in the rear-view mirror as you accelerate, is there lots of blue smoke? Then the engine is very worn, although white steam is normal on a cold morning. Any squeals could simply be a slipping fan belt, which is easy to cure, or that some expensive pumps and bearings could be on their way out. Listen for a whistling turbo, which could be very worn, especially if it takes an age to accelerate and there is lots of smoke pouring from the rear.

After the drive look at the engine bay and underneath. Are there lots of leaks? Is there steam? Burning smells? Don't make an instant decision about the car yet, go away and think about it. Take the Buyer's Companion (see pages 145–151) you have completed and read it carefully. Try and contact the previous owner mentioned on the V5 and also the last garage to do any servicing work, and ask what condition it was in the last time they saw it.

Buying the Car

Make Your Mind Up Time

Only you will know whether the car is worth taking any further. Look at your Buyer's Companion (see pages 145–151). If there are lots of noises noted, the car looks awful and the history is patchy, then it is probably not worth bothering with. If you are uncertain about the seller never be afraid to turn your back on a car, because there will be plenty of others to look at and you don't want to make an expensive mistake. If the car is clean, tidy and according to your Buyer's Companion checklist looks a reasonable prospect, then to avoid making a serious and expensive mistake, it is time to pay for a professional engineer's inspection (see Useful Information, pages 153–5). They will give a written report on the car's condition, a valuation and most carry out independent checks to make sure that the car is not stolen, an insurance write-off, or still subject to a finance agreement. Remember if you inspect the car, or someone does so on your behalf, the dealer is not liable for any faults that you should have uncovered.

How to Haggle

Everyone expects you to do it. That is why advertisements say 'ono', meaning 'or near offer'. Sellers who advertise cars at £4,995 will really take several hundred less. Everyone, both private seller and dealer, builds some flexibility into the price. It pays, though, to be polite and to know what you are doing.

Price

Know what the car is really worth. *Parker's* price guide will tell you and so will looking at lots of similar cars advertised in the local paper. You want to pay the lowest possible figure. Remember that dealers can offer all sorts of facilities such as finance, warranties and often a service before sale, while a private seller offers no protection or benefits – yet often private cars can be very expensive.

Target price

Decide what you want to pay, say £3,500. If the asking price is £3,995 start at a low £3,000. The seller might say £3,750 is the lowest he or she will go, but then you can say, let's meet halfway. It isn't always as simple as that, but if you have a plan you stand a better chance of getting a good deal. Never hesitate, or look embarrassed: just ask for the best price politely and directly, then shut up. If the seller, especially a private one, is desperate to sell, they will do all the babbling and talk themselves into the deal.

Haggling tips

Haggle in hundreds of pounds, never tens or twenties. Dealers appreciate the direct approach. Say you want to do a deal and need to buy a car that day. Be blunt, but still polite. Don't be too eager to buy the particular car you are interested in. Suggest that you will be looking elsewhere. Always be prepared simply to walk away if you don't get the deal you want. Many private sellers and a lot of dealers will crumble at the sight of a certain sale walking away. With a dealer, try to find the sales manager and deal direct with him or her. Remember that car dealers are called dealers for one simple reason: they like to deal. Never, ever pay the asking price.

The Deal

Once you have agreed the price and terms, get it all written down on a piece of paper: details of the car (such as the model), and the parties' names, addresses and telephone numbers. Anything that the seller has agreed to do, such as get something fixed – make sure it is written down and made a term of the contract. Also, get them to write on the paper that, to their knowledge, the car is not stolen, a write-off, or still subject to finance. Also, if you plan to have a professional inspection, then make that a condition of the sale by writing it on the contract – 'This agreement is subject to the vehicle passing an independent vehicle inspection.'

DEALS *on* **WHEELS**

Top Fifty

Used cars, there are millions to choose from and thousands of models. So, how did we manage to narrow it done to our top fifty? With great difficulty. Cars last longer and perform better than ever before. The majority of models launched in the last decade, provided they are looked after, don't give their new, or subsequent, owners much to worry about.

In certain cases it was very easy, because some models pick themselves. In the family car section it's hard to think of a better car than a Ford Mondeo. As for city cars, the much-loved, but seriously dated, Mini may be out-classed by the Fiat Cinquecento, but there are so many Minis around, it is an impossible car to ignore.

We've also tried to cater for the dreamers. Who hasn't pondered a Porsche 911, or even a classic Morris Minor, as they have scanned the classified ads? And because there will never be enough room for every single model in each category, check out some of the more obvious Alternatively ... (see pages 132–42).

There is something for everyone in our top fifty and just maybe your next used car will be here.

Fiat Cinquecento
1993–98

CHECKPOINTS

- Parking dents ◆ Scrapes on bodywork and wheels/tyres
- Leaking sunroof ◆ Shabby interior trim ◆ Tired, smoking engine

Cinquecento profile

Fiat's baby three-door hatchback at just 10' 7" long and 4' 9" wide is the perfectly sized city car. Interior room is limited, but that's not surprising. Sporting version rivals Mini Cooper. The Polish-built Cinquecento is cheap, economical and generally reliable. Very much at home in packed city streets.

 Image ✦✦✦✦✦

Fiat are one of the few manufacturers who genuinely understand what makes a great small car. The most important factors are practicality and styling. A Fiat badge on the front gives the Cinquecento instant credibility and its cheeky charm will win everyone over.

 Running costs ✦✦✦✦✦

The whole point of the Cinquecento is its tiny running costs. A good place to begin is the insurance groups, starting at 2. Even the Sporting gets no higher than 3. Servicing is straightforward and should be cheap. Not difficult to resell, provided the Cinquecento is in tidy condition.

Reliability ●●●○○

The Cinquecento is a cheap car and feels it. Needs to be looked after to give its best, otherwise cold winter starts are a problem. Feels flimsy and can suffer from minor electrical upsets, but on the whole pretty reliable.

 Value for money ●●●○○

Specification is basic, but that is their appeal. Has the bare essentials, which are all most owners need. Cheap interior. Guaranteed not to corrode for eight years from new.

 Comfort ●●●○○

Most city cars are two-seaters and the Cinquecento is no exception. In the front it is possible to get two large adults, but the rear is strictly kids' stuff. Not that refined, with quite stiff suspension, which means you bounce into and out of pot-holes. Again, part of the appeal. Engine noise a pain on long-haul journeys.

 Practicality ●●●○○

Has a tiny boot, but perfectly adequate for most shopping trips.

 Driving ●●●●○

The Cinquecento proves to be a very lively little car to drive. The steering is light and precise which means that parking is a doddle. Gear change is not so slick and the brake/clutch/accelerator pedal layout is clumsy and needs getting used to.

 Performance ●●●○○

The standard 900cc engine is adequate, although far from quick. The bigger-engined Sporting is noticeably faster and more enjoyable to drive, especially on the open road, when its higher top speed, over 90mph, and quicker acceleration are useful. Generally the engines are noisy when pushed hard, but they are responsive at low speeds.

 Economy ●●●●●

Average and overall fuel consumption for the 900 is 48 mpg. Even the Sporting manages over 45 mpg, so not many trips to the petrol station.

 Safety ●●●○○

Good brakes, side impact protection and optional driver's air bag mean that the Cinquecento may be small, but it won't be vulnerable.

 Security ●●●○○

Not much in the way of deterrents until 1995, when the vehicle's identification number was etched on the glass and then an electronic engine immobiliser was fitted.

SUM UP

Which model?

There is no denying that this is a stylish little car, which is cheap to buy and run. At its most basic a 900 has plenty of appeal. As a town runabout it is hard to think of a better buy. Sporting is for those who want even more fun. Easy and cheap to buy without being too dated.

FOR Economy. Styling. Charm.

AGAINST Low-quality feel.

DOW RATING
●●●●○

Ford Ka

1996 on

CHECKPOINTS

♦ Parking damage   ♦ Ex-hire cars   ♦ Thrashed engines
♦ Kerbed wheels and tyres   ♦ Uneven tyre wear

Ka profile

Until the Ford Ka came along, city cars only had to be small; they didn't have to be roomy, exciting to drive, or look very stylish. Luckily, the three-door Ka is all these things. Best of all, it isn't just at home in the city; it feels perfectly happy on the open road too. A truly practical little package which is also a low-cost, no-worry Ford.

 Image   ♦♦♦♦♦

You either love or loathe the styling. What is cheeky and radical to some, is planet weird to others, but the Ka can't be ignored, and that's the point. The Ka is conventional in that it does everything a good car should, but the bodywork and equally adventurous interior confirm that it is finally hip to be seen in a Ford.

 Running costs   ♦♦♦♦♦

The cheapest Ford to run – what more do you want? Servicing costs are among the lowest for any current car and insurance is just group 2, except for the top of the range Ka 3, which is 3. Not easy to resell at the moment. Depreciation is proving to be quite steep as the demand for used examples is more than matched by the supply.

Reliability

Ford has a good reputation for building reliable cars and so far there have been no major problems reported with the Ka. Any faults are due to owner abuse, especially if the Ka has been used as a loan or hire car.

 Value for money

The Ka has not been a huge retail success, which means that used and nearly-new examples continue to be very cheap. The basic Ka, though, is well equipped with minimal safety (air bag), security (deadlocks), manoeuvrability (power steering) and practicality (split rear seat). A Ka 3 adds those big-car luxuries, like air-conditioning and CD player.

 Comfort

This is a refined little car with plenty of room in the front and generous headroom. Little noise gets into the cabin, the suspension is smooth and overall it feels like a much more grown-up car. The supportive and comfortable seats help considerably. Rear-seat passengers find it a tight fit though.

 Practicality

Best used as transport for two, the load space in the boot is not too bad, and the split rear seat is easy to operate.

 Driving

Not a powerful car, but it makes up for this with its agility. The high level of grip and sharp steering puts a real sense of fun back into driving. But when required to cruise, it is quiet, efficient and very relaxing. The perfect combination around town and, remarkably for a small car, at home on longer journeys.

 Performance

The Ka is not quick. The 1.3 engine easily keeps up with town traffic and works well with a slick gear change. 60 mph takes almost 14 seconds to arrive and top speed is just over 90 mph, but for 99 per cent of Ka owners, that is all the performance they will ever need.

 Economy

Fuel consumption overall is just under 50 mpg, so the Ka should cost peanuts to run.

 Safety

Standard safety spec includes a driver's air bag, although a passenger air bag and ABS brakes are extras.

 Security

The Ka is very secure with an engine immobiliser and, most important of all, deadlocks.

SUM UP

Which model?

Basic Ka did not get standard power steering until 1997, although it's always standard on Ka 2. An essential feature for resale purposes. Ka 3 has excellent levels of equipment and at the right low price would be a great buy. All Kas are great and getting cheaper all the time.

FOR Styling. Handling. Comfort.

AGAINST Styling for some. Slow.

DOW RATING
★★★★★

Mini

1959 on

CHECKPOINTS

- ◆ Rust, especially on older models ◆ Oil leaks ◆ Water leaks
- ◆ Collapsed suspension ◆ Smoking, worn-out engine

Mini profile

Cramped, noisy, unrefined and old-fashioned. State of the art in 1959, 40 years later the two-door Mini is falling apart as an argument for city transport. A nearly-new Mini is expensive, but an older one is likely to be cheap, economical and never less than stylish. Fun to drive and mostly fun to own too. A British institution that refuses to go away.

 Image ✦✦✦✦✦

Legendary and lovable: that's the Mini's enduring appeal. You can't argue with the styling, or the sheer fun of driving one. A Mini makes everyone smile. Utterly classless, but a very classy package. Doesn't look 40 years old. Survives because it is a unique classic.

 Running costs ✦✦✦✦✧

Service bills are cheap and so are parts. Tons of second-hand spares too, and can be maintained on a tiny budget. Some garage jobs are easier to do than others and the increasingly high-tech engine is more complex since 1996. Overall, easy and cheap to run.

Reliability

As Minis have become more complicated, they do go wrong more often. Electrics, oil leaks and gearboxes are weak spots and can cause trouble, but no major flaw in this well-proven design. Hard-used examples have to be looked after.

Value for money

Nearly-new Minis, despite 90s updates, are bad value because of the low comfort and refinement levels. Older, cheaper Minis are the ultimate in basic transportation and deliver the cheap thrills they promise.

Comfort

An occupational hazard of being on board such a small, old car is the jerky ride. The seats are well padded, but unsupportive, the engine and gearbox noise is intrusive. A bad idea on motorway journeys, bearable around town.

Practicality

Tiny boot, although back seats useful for luggage. Seats four surprisingly well on short journeys.

Driving

Dated 60s driving position and controls. On the road lots of grip. It won't fall over, however hard you drive. Sporty and fun.

Performance

Minis always feel faster than they really are. Adequate power from the most recent 1.3 engine. Older 1000s 1.0 litre is slow but sure. The secret of driving a Mini fast is to keep up the momentum on bends rather than flat-out speeds. Not really happy on motorways.

Economy

All Minis manage 40 mpg as a minimum and the older 1000 gets almost 50 mpg. Despite its tiny fuel tank the Mini manages to feel as though it runs forever before it needs filling up. Oil consumption can be on the high side though, especially with older examples. Modern rivals have better economy, but they never feel as much fun to drive.

Safety

The Mini feels more vulnerable than most. No safety features until 1996, when side impact beams, plus a driver's air bag were fitted. The Mini's quick handling should help get a driver out of trouble.

Security

Never very difficult to break into, the Mini range has only recently (1996) been fitted with an engine immobiliser and alarm. Before that, nothing.

SUM UP

Which model?

It is difficult to justify spending a lot of money on a nearly-new Mini when there are so many much more modern small cars to choose from. But a tidy and cheap example which is ten years old would make an ideal first car, or fabulous runabout.

FOR Handling. Heritage. Style. Economy.

AGAINST Dated. Cramped. Uncomfortable.

DOW RATING

Peugeot 205

1983 on

CHECKPOINTS

♦ Rust on early models ♦ Oil leaks ♦ Smoky and noisy high mileage engines, especially diesels ♦ Shabby interior trim ♦ Parking damage

205 profile

Back in the early 80s the 205 set the small hatchback standard. A range of three- and five-door hatches and later a two-door cabriolet managed to combine fuel economy with a stylish design, reliable engines and great handling. They now represent great value as a cheap and cheerful runabout.

 Image

The 205 still manages to cut a dash on the streets. The GTI in particular is an icon. Design has barely dated at all and it has so much more character than most hatches. It can do the shopping run, but remains a stylish and chic alternative to something much more boring.

 Running costs

Insurance is cheap at just group 4. The engines, provided no major work is needed, are simple to service, parts are cheap and there are plentiful second-hand spares. Running a 205 on a tight budget is not a problem. Reselling a good one isn't, either. Diesel versions cost more to insure.

Reliability ●●●○○

The 205 has proved to be reliable, although earlier cars are much more troublesome now if they have been neglected. Engines are quite tough, but the build quality is on the flimsy side. Bits of interior trim can fall off and the body panels feel tinny.

 Value for money ●●●○○

Early examples can be picked up for hundreds of pounds now and will either soldier on for years without complaint, or be a pile of trouble. That is the risk you run with every car. However, a tidy 205 which has been looked after will be a cheap and reliable workhorse.

 Comfort ●●●●○

The driving position is very good in the 205, the seats in particular are very supportive. Much is made of the car's suspension, which means that it soaks up uneven road surfaces like a much bigger car. There is plenty of engine noise and it is a bit cramped in the back.

 Practicality ●●●○○

There is a small but useful boot, a high hatchback loading lip by modern standards. On the whole, a 205 can take a fair amount of luggage/shopping.

 Driving ●●●●●

The whole range of 205s offers the driver a very safe, secure, but fun experience. There is plenty of grip in corners. Good steering at speed, with fine brakes and an easy gear change. Around town, though, the steering can feel a little bit heavy for some. Overall it feels like a much bigger car in the sense of behaviour on the road. The sportiness of even the humblest model is very rewarding.

 Performance ●●●●○

Smallest 1.0 litre is slow and not ideal if you plan to do motorway work, or over-taking. 1.1 is better and the 1.4 and 1.6 engines are even better if the 205 is not going to be town-bound. GTI seriously quick in 1.6 or 1.9 form. Diesel is desperately slow.

 Economy ●●●●●

Small engines get close to 50 mpg, diesel almost 60 mpg. Even the GTIs won't do worse than mid-30s.

 Safety ●●●○○

A solid little car, but with no active safety features apart from optional ABS brakes on some models.

 Security ●●○○○

The 205 has always been easy to break into.

SUM UP

Which model?

1.0s are too slow, 1.1s are great town cars, but the 1.4s are probably the best all-rounders for economy and performance. A five-door will always be more practical and easier to resell. GTIs are great; however, buying a good one is not easy.

FOR Economy. Comfort. GTI performance.

AGAINST Cramped rear. Lots of shabby 205s out there.

DOW RATING
●●●●○

Fiat Punto   1994 on

CHECKPOINTS

♦ Parking damage   ♦ Electrical problems   ♦ Interior trim can be fragile

Punto profile

The Fiat Punto is one of the most spacious small hatchbacks on the market. The styling still looks fresh, the equipment levels are excellent, there is a wide range of models and, overall, the practical Punto is a great all-round package. They are becoming cheaper to buy too. One of the best hatchbacks of the 90s.

 Image   ●●●●○

Punto is a classless car. Accepted anywhere and recognised as having a style and Italian flair which lift it above other more ordinary hatches, the Punto can be forgiven small niggly faults. Basically, the Punto has bags of character. Not everyone likes the shape although it hasn't dated much at all.

 Running costs   ●●●●○

Reassuringly inexpensive to run. Insurance groupings start at 3 and for all mainstream models never exceed 5. Only the GT gets pricey at 14. Servicing is reasonably priced, provided no big parts are needed, which can cost lots. Currently an easy model to resell, so depreciation not too steep.

Reliability ●●●○○

Fiat's reputation for building reliable cars increased with the introduction of the Punto, which proved they could make solid hatchbacks. Minor electrical problems and weak interior trim aside, the Punto has no major weaknesses provided it is not abused.

 Value for money ●●●○○

Fiat specification lists are not overgenerous, but then the Punto is intended as a cheap practical car. SX and ELX models improve specification levels. Lots of Puntos are coming off company fleets now, and that means prices are reasonable and the choice is wide.

 Comfort ●●●○○

The Punto is very roomy in leg and head departments, although the seats are not that supportive. However, the trim material is on the cheap side. The suspension is very firm and surprisingly can prove less than comfortable in town over poorly repaired roads.

 Practicality ●●●○○

Although the Punto has a good boot and lots of interior space, a split rear seat is not standard until higher up the range. Plenty of room for four adults. The big doors in the three-door make access to the rear easy and the low loading lip on the hatch is also extremely useful.

 Driving ●●●●○

Excellent driving position in the Punto; the large glass area helps and overall it is safe and predictable. Cornering creates notice-able body roll, despite there being plenty of grip. Power steering around town is a must for most drivers.

 Performance ●●●○○

The smallest engines are most suited to the Punto's practical character. The 1.1 and 1.2 are very eager, especially the Sporting. The 1.4 Turbo GT is exciting, and gets to 60 mph in around eight seconds, but the turbo delivers the power too suddenly on occasions. The turbo diesel engine is slow, but frugal.

 Economy ●●●●○

Over 40 mpg for the smallest petrol engines, although the diesels will get around 47 mpg. Even the high-performance turbo still manages 33 mpg.

 Safety ●●●●○

All models come with pre-tensioner seat-belts although a driver's air bag is an extra on most models, as are ABS brakes.

 Security ●●●○○

Fiat's key immobiliser system is standard from 1995 models, some models have remote central locking and an alarm.

SUM UP

Which model?

Find the highest specification model you can and the 75 ELX, or more powerful 85 ELX. Power steering always worth having. Turbo is probably best avoided.

FOR Roomy. Stylish. Comfortable.

AGAINST Poor ride.

DOW RATING
●●●●○

Ford Fiesta 1989–96

CHECKPOINTS

- ◆ Rust ◆ Oil leaks ◆ Worn clutch and gearbox ◆ Thrashed XR2s
- ◆ Accident and parking damage ◆ Worn suspension ◆ Shabby interiors

Fiesta profile

The old Fiesta really does seem dated when compared with the latest model. This three- and five-door hatch represents an affordable option for those after a tough, reliable and practical car which will be very cheap to run. A sound budget buy.

 Image ●●●○○

Honest and working-class is the only way to describe the old Fiesta. There is nothing flash or remarkable about this style-free, but solid little car. The XR2 provides some glamour, but the image is pure hooligan unfortunately. All other versions, though, are respectable enough.

 Running costs ●●●●○

At the heart of this old car's appeal is the fact that it is very easy to service. Parts prices are very low and the second-hand spares market is highly developed. Probably the cheapest used car to run at the moment in terms of maintaining a tight budget without compromising reliability, or safety.

Reliability ✸✸✸○○

Not a great deal to go wrong with such a simple car. Older examples can prove problematic if neglected. Wear and tear on the components are the major reasons for failures, but at least the parts are cheap to replace.

Value for money ✸✸✸○○

Can be cheap to buy; however, there are lots of shabby Fiestas on sale. Tidy cars hold their value well, but avoid the most basic models and aim for better-value LX and Ghia.

Comfort ✸✸○○○

Not the most relaxing small car to drive. The engines are noisy and the driving position is not adjustable, especially for the smaller driver. Feels cramped inside too, rear-seat passengers are very badly served. On top of all that, the suspension gives a bouncy and uncomfortable ride.

Practicality ✸✸✸✸○

There is a small but useful boot. Most of all, this is a very easy car to own, especially in five-door format.

Driving ✸✸✸○○

Distinctly average to drive. Not very refined at all. Makes jerky progress due to a sticky gear change, steering which feels a little vague and a noisy range of engines. It is bearable, rather than enjoyable.

Performance ✸✸✸○○

Older and smaller engines are not very good; 1.0 litre is too slow, 1.1 not much better. 1.4 from 1994 best of all, although not many around − otherwise try the 1.3.

1.6 is the performance option, try the S model rather than XR2 or turbo. Diesel slow and noisy.

Economy ✸✸✸✸○

1.1 returns between 45 and 49 mpg. 1.3 manages over 40 mpg and the diesel is an easy 50 mpg. On the whole mpg is very good.

Safety ✸✸✸○○

Average safety features up until 1994, when the Fiesta was thoroughly uprated as the body was strengthened, plus side impact protection beams and driver's air bag were fitted as standard.

Security ✸✸○○○

Very easy to break into. Again, 1994 is the year when the Fiesta got some important improvements, which included an engine immobiliser.

SUM UP

Which model?

Avoid 1.0 litre and any 1.1 models with a four-speed gearbox. Five-door are easier to resell, and remember that from May 1994 there were important safety and security upgrades. 1.3 and especially 1.4 engines are the best all-rounders.

FOR Practical. Economical. Lots to choose from.

AGAINST Uncomfortable. Unrefined. Noisy. Some nasty ones on sale.

DOW RATING
✸✸✸○○

Ford Fiesta   1995 on

CHECKPOINTS

♦ Engine oil leaks   ♦ Parking damage to wheel trims and tyres, plus the painted bumpers and door rubbing strips   ♦ Service history

Fiesta profile

Latest and best Fiesta launched in 1995. In terms of comfort and performance, this is now the class-leading small hatch. The Ford badge means ownership is easy because dealers are nearby and running costs low. It may be a bit cramped in the rear and in the boot, but the latest Fiesta is safe, reliable and the most sensible used buy.

 Image

The Fiesta remains a tough and hard-working little car; however, the sheer numbers around mean that it won't ever go upmarket. The latest Fiesta is modern, efficient and practical, although not every-one likes the styling, or thinks it is as chic as some European rivals.

 Running costs

Servicing costs are low and can get even lower when the Fiesta is out of warranty, because every garage can service them. Insurance costs are low as the 1.3 litre-engined cars start at group 3. Service intervals are every 10,000 miles, which for most owners means one garage visit a year.

Reliability ●●●●○

Fiestas are well built. However, the 1.25 engine needs careful servicing and there are occasional electrical niggles, but nothing serious provided the car is looked after.

  Value ●●●○○

Getting more affordable now, although Ford dealers are the most expensive places to buy. Made in large numbers, so becomes cheaper quicker, but long-term it is always an easy model to resell.

  Comfort ●●●●●

Front-seat passengers have lots of room, although those in the rear are not so lucky, especially if they have to squeeze past the front seat in a three-door. Big-car ride comfort, though, as the bumps are easily soaked up.

  Practicality ●●●○○

Luggage room suffers because the rear suspension intrudes into the boot.

  Driving ●●●●●

There is a clearly laid-out dashboard and, although the steering wheel does not adjust, the position is very comfortable. On the road, the body hardly rolls on tight corners, the steering is precise and responsive. Easy to drive in town.

  Performance ●●●●○

Best engines are the 1.25 and 1.4 units. The larger engine has a sportier set-up, but the 1.25 offers similar levels of performance, being eager but never sounding overworked. Entry-level 1.3 is old, sounds rough and the 1.8 diesel is noisy, slow and unrefined.

  Economy ●●●●○

42.2 mpg is the average overall fuel consumption for the smaller 1.25 and 1.3 engines. The 1.4 manages 38.9 and the diesel 47.9.

  Safety ●●●●○

The Fiesta has scored highly in European crash tests and a driver's air bag is standard. Passenger air bag and ABS brakes are options on some models.

  Security ●●●●○

The Fiesta has scored consistently high marks in independent security tests. An engine immobiliser is standard, but a very secure deadlock system and alarm are only options. Visible vehicle identification numbers (VINs) are included across the range.

SUM UP

Which model?

Like all Fords there are lots of trim options, although the standard specification is reasonable. The fact that the Fiesta is such a good all-round car makes it good value anyway, but the 1.25 LX versions have the best combination of engine and specification and will be the easiest to resell.

FOR Easy to drive. Comfort. Handling. Engines.

AGAINST Boot and rear space. Diesel.

```
DOW RATING
   ●●●●○
```

Nissan Micra 1993 on

C H E C K P O I N T S

◆ Noisy engine at high mileage ◆ Ex-driving school Micras lead hard
lives ◆ Look for parking dents ◆ Slipping clutches

Micra profile

Nissan's British-built three- and five-door hatchbacks have always been among
the best-built and most able in their class. Revised model (1998) has been
updated in terms of performance, styling and specification. Practical and easy
to own, the Micra may still fall just short of latest Ford Fiesta but it remains
a sensible choice.

 Image ●●●●○

Not everyone likes the toytown styling.
There is a fine line between chic and cute,
and even though Nissan claim to have
beefed up the appearance in 1998, it still
looks a bit too cute. Otherwise the Micra is
taken seriously as an A-to-B errand-runner.
Nissan no longer means cheap and nasty,
but well built and refined.

 **Running
costs** ●●●○○

Nissan do not break the first rule of small
cars, which is to make the service costs
small. Easy to work on and with good parts
availability, not as expensive to run as
some Japanese cars. Low insurance, just
group 3 for a 1.0 litre. Resale value is
always good because demand for well-
looked-after Micras is so strong.

Reliability

Provided the Micra is serviced according to schedule, there is unlikely to be a problem. Only owner-inflicted abuse and neglect cause any trouble, otherwise faultless.

 ## Value for money

There are plenty of Micras to choose from now, which means that prices are reasonable, particularly the entry-level 1.0 models. Nissan dealers are expensive, but lots at supermarket sites now. In safety and security terms, the Micra scores highly. There may even be the balance of its new three-year, 60,000 mile warranty.

 ## Comfort

The 1998 interior restyle has made the Micra look more modern, but it can still feel a bit narrow; even so, the head- and legroom are very good. Great seats. Under most conditions the ride is smooth, but can feel less so when out on the open road.

 ## Practicality

Luggage space is adequate enough without being overgenerous. Worry-free nature and refinement of the Micra make it practical.

 ## Driving

Unlike some small hatches, the Micra does not really have a sporting nature. It always feels safe and secure, although the body rolls a fair bit on corners. Ideally the Micra prefers to stay in town with its light and easy controls, plus a tight turning circle. It never feels less than nimble.

 ## Performance

The 1.0 litre unit is fine for most urban duties, it is slow, but does not feel it,

getting to 60 mph in over sixteen seconds. Push it hard and that engine also starts to sound harsh. If you plan on regular long-distance or motorway driving, then the 1.3 is more lively. Automatic transmission is the best of its type.

 ## Economy

1.0 litre manages 47 mpg and even the 1.3 litre manages 46 mpg. Excellent. In small-car terms, and especially for one as refined as the Micra, the fuel economy is exceptional.

 ## Safety

Driver's air bag is standard on the majority of the range from 1995. Passenger air bag is optional across most of the other models. ABS brakes likewise are optional.

 ## Security

Engine immobilisers since 1996. Not much protection on early models. Easy to break into unless fitted with a deadlock system. This was added in 1998.

SUM UP

Which model?

One of the best of the small hatches. Styling not for everyone, but a 1.3 five-door would be the best all-round choice, especially a post-1995 example with important security and safety upgrades.

FOR Comfort. Reliability. Refinement. Economy.

AGAINST Hardly anything. Styling?

DOW RATING
●●●●○

Peugeot 106 1991 on

CHECKPOINTS

- ◆ Noisy engine   ◆ Clutch worn   ◆ Oil leaks   ◆ Interior trim damage
- ◆ Uneven tyre wear   ◆ Parking damage   ◆ Ex-driving school?

106 profile

Peugeot produced a class-leading three- and five-door hatchback in 1991, but despite some important revisions in recent years, it isn't quite as roomy or well built as something like a VW Polo. However, the 106 is never less than fun to drive and remains one of the better small hatches on sale today.

Image ●●●●○

There is no denying that the 106 is a very pretty little hatchback, more so than the Citroen Saxo, which is basically the same car under the body. Peugeot have a fine reputation for building innovative and practical small cars. They also build great-handling cars, and GTI and Rallye versions really look the performance-car part.

Running costs ●●●●○

The 106 is relatively cheap to service and when it comes to spares most other costs are reasonable too. Insurance grouping starts at 3. Resale values are consistent and strong. Everyone wants an old 106, it seems so a 106 is certainly worth looking after in order to keep the depreciation to a minimum.

Reliability ●●●○○

Peugeots are much better built than they used to be, and there are just a few build quality shortfalls, which mean that it may not feel as solid as other small hatches. No major problems; the 106 just needs regular servicing.

Value for money ●●●○○

Lots of 106s to choose from. Prices rise significantly for the 1996 models, when the range was upgraded. Increasing numbers of nearly new 106s around. Entry-level XNs have very basic specifications.

Comfort ●●●○○

There is not a great deal of room in a 106. Rear space is at a premium – even in the front it can feel a bit tight, especially for taller drivers who have to cope with restricted headroom and controls which are offset to the left. Never mind, at least the 106 offers a superb ride over the roughest tarmac.

Practicality ●●●○○

Easy to live with, but compared to so many other hatches it feels too small.

Driving ●●●●●

Most drivers will enjoy the sharp steering, balance and poise of the whole 106 package. From the humblest XN to the hot GTI, no 106 is a disappointment. Arguably the GTI is the best small hot hatch you can buy. Around town doing the shopping it is light and nimble. The perfect combination.

Performance ●●●●●

Early 1.0 engine is too slow. However, the 1.1 and 1.4 petrol units are lively and accelerate eagerly, even if they get much more noisy at speed. The 1.5 litre diesel is refined and also quite brisk, while the GTI's 1.6 sprints to 60 mph in less than eight seconds.

Economy ●●●●○

Fuel consumption for the smallest 1.1 and 1.4 are over 40 mpg, diesels over 50 mpg and the performance GTI mid-30s. The 106 has a wonderful ability to stretch a gallon of fuel further than many other similar cars because it is so light.

Safety ●●●○○

There is no air bag on the lowest models, although this was optional from 1993. Much stronger body from 1996, with side impact beams and seatbelt pre-tensioners.

Security ●●●○○

Peugeot's keypad engine-immobiliser system is standard across the range from 1996, this can be annoying as you have to enter a code. There is an optional alarm on some models and most have remote central locking.

SUM UP

Which model?

Avoid XNs where the specification is just too basic, and also the 1.0 engine. 1996 is an important year for safety and security upgrades. GTI and Rallye offer lots of fun.

FOR Fuel economy. Driving pleasure.

AGAINST On the small side.

DOW RATING
●●●●○

Renault Clio 1991 on

CHECKPOINTS

♦ Electrical problems: check wipers and heater
♦ Engine difficult to start when cold or damp ♦ Parking damage
♦ Uneven tyre wear ♦ Smoking diesel and petrol engines

Clio profile

Stylish and successful, the three- and five-door Clio became one of the most successful small hatches before being thoroughly revised in 1998. The latest is undoubtedly fine value, safer and better-handling than before, but the interior space is limited and engines are mostly the old ones. The older Clio is now a great-value used buy.

 Image ●●●●●

The Clio has one of the strongest small-hatch images around. It is still chic and very distinctive, thanks to, or possibly in spite of, Nicole and her Papa. The Clio has taken over from where the old Renault 5 left off, making it one of the smarter small cars to be seen in.

 Running costs ●●●○○

Insurance ratings start low at group 3. Resale value is still strong for the right clean and tidy examples. Parts prices are average, rather than cheap, although a large number of second-hand spares are around now from specialists. Some servicing jobs not ideal for the DIY mechanic.

Reliability ●●●○○

Clio is home to small niggly faults, mainly in the electrical department. Heaters and wipers can go on the blink. The engine needs to be kept in tune, otherwise there are hot and cold starting problems. Overall, though, a pretty good record provided there's not a high mileage, or it's an abused example.

  ### Value for money ●●●●○

The arrival of the new Clio in 1998 has meant that the old one has dropped in price. Lots around, and mainly with private sellers. If they have a full service history and are in tidy condition, these are the ideal Clios to buy.

  ### Comfort ●●●○○

The interior is plasticky and a bit cheap, but it is light and gives the feeling of spaciousness, even if it only seats four at a squeeze. Seats are a bit too soft, but on the move the ride and refinement levels are very good, whether in town, or out on the open road.

  ### Practicality ●●●○○

Reasonable boot and easy driveability of the Clio makes it very practical as an everyday car. The later-model Clio provides a welcome boost to luggage and general storage space inside the car.

  ### Driving ●●●●○

The Clio is in its element around town. Light steering, even without power assistance, combines with a smooth gear change for rapid progress. The enthusiastic driver will find plenty of grip and nicely balanced steering on the open road. Brakes could be a little firmer.

  ### Performance ●●●●○

1.2 engine is smooth and eager, but not that quick, although it is ideally suited to a town-bound Clio. The 1.4 has more power for motorway work. There is a noisy, old but adequate diesel. 1.8 is the fast option especially in 16V form. The 2.0 Williams models are not for the faint-hearted.

  ### Economy ●●●○○

50 mpg from the 1.2 is on a par with the diesel. 40 mpg from the 1.4.

  ### Safety ●●●○○

Not many safety features until optional air bags in 1994. Revised models in 1996 had a stronger body with most models getting a standard air bag.

  ### Security ●●●○○

Easy to steal, immobilisers across the range only from 1996 and alarms on performance Clios.

SUM UP

Which model?

1.4 model the best all-rounder. 1996 models saw big safety and security improvements. Avoid early 1.2s, which have inadequate four-speed gearboxes. Power steering standard on RT model from 1994.

FOR Easy to drive. Spacious.

AGAINST Basic versions. Electrical niggles.

DOW RATING
●●●○○

Vauxhall Nova
1983–92

CHECKPOINTS

♦ Rust around boot and on wings ♦ Water leaks ♦ Engine noisy and oil leaks ♦ Worn gearboxes and clutch ♦ Parking damage

Nova profile

Boxy and dated by now, but proving to be an enduring favourite on the used-car market. This range of three- and five-door hatchbacks, plus an unpopular saloon, has plenty to offer those who want to run a car on a tight budget. Easy to work on, very economical and with lots to choose from, the Nova is a sound banger buy.

Image   ●●○○○

Never stylish, especially when compared to the Peugeot 205, the Nova remains a hard grafter. Dated design, downmarket Vauxhall badge and low comfort levels don't get in the way of the facts: the Nova is dirt cheap.

Running costs   ●●●●●

Group 3 insurance, only the sporty versions get pricey. Servicing could not be easier. Any decent garage and any competent DIY mechanic could cope. Lots of second-hand spares and Vauxhall specialists to help. Ideal first car.

Reliability ●●●●○

Simplicity of the design means that there is not a lot to go wrong. Major Vauxhall components are very durable. Only very old and neglected Novas give any real trouble.

  Value for money ●●●●○

Although it is becoming harder to find pristine Novas, they do exist with careful private owners. Prices are generally low and there are still a lot to choose from in the local classified advertisements. If you don't need a hatchback, the unloved saloon version is even cheaper.

  Comfort ●●○○○

This is not a Nova priority. The engine is noisy, road noise is intrusive and the small car's ride is rough. At least the front seats are supportive. Those unlucky enough to be in the rear are going to feel cramped. Overall, pretty unrefined.

  Practicality ●●●○○

Small boot, but the Nova remains a very usable little car for local errands.

  Driving ●●●○○

The Nova is a competent car on the road. Around town it may be a rough diamond, but the controls and steering, which was never power-assisted, are light and easy to use. Quite fun on the open road too.

  Performance ●●●○○

Small engines like the 1.0 and 1.2 really are very slow, although the 1.2 is the better bet. 1.4 is much more lively, 1.5 diesel not worth the bother, although turbo diesel is quicker than most of the petrols. SRI and GSI are quick.

  Economy ●●●○○

Across the Nova range, all models manage over 40 mpg. Diesels are well into the 50s. 1.2 is the best performance/economy combination. This is one of the explanations why the Nova is still so highly sought after and why running costs are kept to a minimum.

  Safety ●○○○○

Design shows its age with no obvious safety features fitted during its life, apart from seatbelts. Although the Nova is not state of the art for safety there is no reason to panic about its performance should you crash.

  Security ●○○○○

Easy car to steal and no factory-fitted deterrents either. Security measures are up to the owners. One of the most vulnerable cars on sale and that causes problems because the Nova is highly sought after for parts.

SUM UP

Which model?

The Nova is a great banger. Don't buy models that are too old and worn out, though. Aim for at least a 1.2, avoid the diesel and try to find a late 1.4 for some degree of refinement, especially if the Nova gets used for regular long trips.

FOR Cheapness. Economy. Simplicity.

AGAINST Cramped. Noisy.

```
DOW RATING
●●●○○
```

Vauxhall Corsa
1993 on

C H E C K P O I N T S

◆ Minor rust   ◆ Poor paintwork   ◆ Worn clutches   ◆ Parking damage
◆ Ex-driving-school cars   ◆ Engine problems with 1.4 16V

Corsa profile

One of the biggest-selling cars in its class is the three- and five-door. The smallest
Vauxhall is practical, roomy, economical and comfortable, yet it falls short of
many rivals because it lacks refinement and can never be described as fun to drive.
Competent, cute and around in large numbers, so plenty to choose from.

 Image   ●●●○○

The Corsa still manages to make onlookers
go 'ah'. Cheeky styling always helps a small
car become accepted. The packaging of the
Corsa is pretty much perfect; and it is ideally
suited to school run and shopping duties.
Small and stylish it may be, even though the
Vauxhall badge and name are hardly chic.

 Running costs   ●●●●○

Low running costs? Corsa has them. Just
group 2 insurance for a start. Low service
and parts costs too. Depreciation about
average for what is a mass-produced car,
but there is always a strong demand,
especially for tidy five-door models. So
short- and long-term, cost effective.

Reliability ●●●○○

There have been some teething problems with Vauxhall's baby, mainly related to build quality and electrics. Also some 1.4 engines have reacted badly to certain unleaded fuel. Sounds worse than it really is; overall Corsa is OK if serviced properly.

 Value for money ●●●○○

Lots around, although buyers have to choose carefully and avoid ex-hire cars and driving-school cars. Entry-level Merit models are very poorly equipped, so it is always best to aim high, and find at least a GLS model.

 Comfort ●●●●○

Whether it is a three- or five-door, there is plenty of room inside a Corsa, which also has particularly comfortable seats. The Corsa lets its passengers down on ride and refinement. Bumps get transferred to the cabin and it feels restless.

 Practicality ●●●●○

Well-thought-out interior means a reasonable boot, and a useful amount of storage space inside.

 Driving ●●●○○

Good news because of the excellent driving position and clearly laid-out dashboard. However, Corsa falls short when it comes to driver enjoyment; under normal urban conditions the Corsa feels, well, rather coarse, which is a shame. Improvements in 1997 have helped a bit.

 Performance ●●●○○

There is a wide choice of engines. The 1.0 litre three-cylinder engine is sluggish, taking almost twenty seconds to 60 mph, but offers remarkable economy. In fact, the 1.2 and 1.4 engines offer little real performance improvement and only the 16-valve 1.4 fitted to the Sport is quick. All other engines are slow, unrefined and noisy.

 Economy ●●●○○

Major fuel consumption boost as the 1.0 litre petrol just falls short of 50 mpg, whereas the diesel manages just over that figure.

 Safety ●●●○○

Air bags are not standard except on GLS models, although the CDX also has a passenger air bag. ABS brakes are optional on most models.

 Security ●●●●○

Lower down the Corsa range, protection is marginal, apart from an engine immobiliser. Excellent deadlock system only on GLS models and larger-engined models. Alarm only on Sport and CDX.

SUM UP

Which model?

1997 was the year the range was substantially revised. It pays to choose carefully by specification. Power steering, air bag and five doors will all help at resale time. Small engine sluggish, so 1.4 is the best all rounder.

FOR Styling. Economy. Practicality.

AGAINST Handling. Refinement.

DOW RATING
●●●●○

Volkswagen Polo
1994 on

CHECKPOINTS

♦ Service history ♦ Oil leaks ♦ Parking damage ♦ Worn clutch

Polo profile

Volkswagen reinvented the supermini. According to them, it ought to be high-quality, refined and stylish. Result: the Polo. There is a roomy interior, strong engines and a wide choice. VW have rebadged some Polo-based Spanish-built SEATs to broaden the range, with a saloon and estate models.

 Image ✦✦✦✦✦

The majority of VWs have a sky-high reputation and lots of respect. The Polo may be at the cheaper end of their range, but all those important VW qualities remain intact. Classy styling sets it apart from many rivals, looks solid and likely to last well into the millennium. No one ever made a mistake by choosing to buy a used Polo.

 Running costs ✦✦✦✦✦

Cheapest VW to own, with servicing and parts among the lowest. Insurance group starts at just number 3. Depreciation is very slow and has one of the best resale values in its class. A good short- or long-term prospect. A Polo makes sound financial sense as either a second car or as main transportation.

Reliability ●●●●●

Just a few early build quality problems with the ignition, but on the whole, utterly reliable if maintained properly.

  Value for money ●●●○○

Cheap for a VW, but not easy to buy as a cheap used car. Basic 1.0 litre is very basic. Payback time is when the Polo is sold, though, with strong demand and prices. May still have balance of brand new three-year unlimited mileage warranty.

  Comfort ●●●●○

Sizeable inside, dark trim although quality material, may depress some occupants. Refinement is what makes the Polo such a pleasure. Road noise is minimal and the ride is supple and smooth.

  Practicality ●●●●○

Big door bins and centre console, but passenger glovebox goes if an air bag is fitted. Decent boot (huge on the saloon).

  Driving ●●●●●

A good adjustable position, firm but comfy seat and well laid out. Handling is safe and predictable. At its best when travelling securely down the motorway, or soaking up the bumps around town. Light controls make it easy to drive.

  Performance ●●●●○

Standard 1.4 is fine, and even the entry-level 1.0 litre is adequate, but don't expect to do much overtaking. 16-valve 1.4 has added some sportiness to the line-up as 60 mph arrives in just over ten seconds now. 1.9 diesel is noisy but frugal. 1.6 is the most relaxed, but no faster than a 1.4.

  Economy ●●●●○

Fuel consumption never much lower than 39 mpg. Surprising the pre-1996 1.0 litre version is much less fuel efficient than its replacement, when mpg shot up from 41.2 to 47.1. Big fuel returns come from the diesel which almost manages 50 mpg overall. The 1.6 CL returns the worst figures at 36.2 mpg. The higher perform-ance 16V 1.6 is a 40 mpg model and the less powerful 1.6 version manages 42.2 mpg.

  Safety ●●●●○

Driver air bags are standard across the majority of the range except for 1.0 litre hatches. ABS always optional, along with passenger air bags. Scored well in in-dependent crash test. Feels safe and solid too.

  Security ●●●○○

Minimal protection from the VW factory, just an engine immobiliser. Door locks uprated in mid-1997. The Polo is an obvious inner-city target and needs quite a lot of protection to prevent it being a soft touch.

SUM UP

Which model?

It is difficult to lose with a used Polo. All models have their merits, but the 1.4 is the best performance/economy compromise.

FOR Build quality. Refinement.

AGAINST Nothing.

DOW RATING
●●●●●

Rover 100/Metro
1980–98

CHECKPOINTS

♦ Rust especially on earlier models ♦ Oil leaks ♦ Noisy engine
♦ Sagging suspension ♦ Parking damage ♦ Shabby interiors
♦ Electrics on later versions can play up

100/Metro profile

Very old design, but there are so many around and it is still a popular used buy that is difficult to overlook. As a cheap runabout, the Metro and, as it later became, the Rover 100 is very economical to run and quite good fun to drive, being essentially a more practical Mini. Potentially a great budget buy.

 Image ●○○○○

Unfortunately the 100/Metro does not have any. Whereas the Mini keeps its cheeky charm 40 years on, the Metro remains the sort of dull, British car bought by pensioners. Not very hip, then.

 Running costs ●●●●●

Most DIY mechanics can cope with this simple and well-proven car. Lots of cheap second-hand parts and dead ones in scrapyards make it perfect as a first car buy. Insurance costs are minimal.

Reliability ●●●○○

On the whole, Metros prove to be quite reliable. Only at high mileage, or when worn out, do they play up. Later versions have a quite sophisticated engine management system, and that is when electrical bugs can strike.

 Value for money ●●●○○

The Metro is so cheap to buy, and there are so many to choose from. The fact that it is unloved keeps prices at rock bottom. Buying from one careful private owner is the way to do it. Will prove a problem to sell on, though.

 Comfort ●●●○○

Early Metros from the 80s are very poor in this important department with their noisy engines and bouncy ride. Matters have improved steadily over the years – much better from 1990. However, the interior is still cramped, especially at the back.

 Practicality ●●●○○

With the rear seats folded, you can get quite a lot in the back. Three-door is more difficult to live with if you regularly take passengers. Surprisingly effective workhorse.

 Driving ●●●●○

Uncomfortable driving position, very dated dashboard, but like the Mini there is lots of grip and the Metro can be thrown around in complete safety. New suspension from 1990 a big help towards refinement.

 Performance ●●●●○

Older engines from the 80s are noisy, slow and just about adequate. New generation of

units from 1990 a huge improvement. So the 1.1 is eager and the 1.4 is decidedly nippy, although diesel model painfully slow.

 Economy ●●●●○

Diesel does 60 mpg if that is what you need. Otherwise, all models are over 40 mpg and the 1.1 close to 50 mpg.

 Safety ●●●○○

80s models have no safety features. When rebadged in 1995, the Rover 100 got side impact beams and the optional air bag made it safer. Not rated highly. European safety tests condemned the Rover 100 which failed to match 90s standards of crash protection. Remember that this car was designed in the 70s.

 Security ●●○○○

Easy to break into, again Rover 100 was an improvement, with standard engine immobiliser. The big improvements came from 1993, otherwise the early models are extremely vulnerable.

SUM UP

Which model?

Range has to be judged on budget terms and deserves an average three-star rating, although it's really at best a two-star car. Post-1990 models are a class apart from old 80s examples. Rover 100 from 1995, provided it is cheap, is the best of the lot.

FOR Cheap.

AGAINST Cramped.

DOW RATING
●●●○○

Ford Escort

1990 on

CHECKPOINTS

♦ Electrical problems, check that all basic controls,
from wipers to windows, work ♦ Smoking high-mileage engines
♦ Parking dents and body damage ♦ Altered mileages

Escort profile

Perennial UK best-seller, the Escort in five-door hatchback and estate form has proved hugely popular, although the saloon and three-door hatchback, less so. The new generation Escorts arrived in 1990 and were awful. Since then, rather than being crude and dull, it is now solid, comfortable, sort of refined, but still dull. For many, those are still admirable qualities. The right Escort is a safe used buy.

 ### Image ●●●○○

Working-class, always was and always will be. Owners are perceived as being as uncomplicated as the cars, only wanting reliability and rock-bottom running costs. That makes the Escort honest transportation; nothing more, nothing less. Even the credibility-boosting XR3 and Cosworth were discontinued early.

 ### Running costs ●●●●○

The whole point of having an Escort is so that you won't be out of pocket, and it does not disappoint. Servicing costs are low and the insurance group starts at a lowly 4. Resale value, even though the new Focus replacement is around, is still reasonable for the class. Demand for used Escorts will remain strong for some time to come.

Reliability ●●●○○

Escorts have benefited from Ford's much-improved build quality. Despite some niggly problems, the car is no worse than any other in its class when it comes to break-downs and recurring faults. Those built after 1995 are much better than original 1990 cars. September 1992 also saw a lot of important revisions, which made those models better too.

 ## Value for money ●●●●○

Huge numbers of Escorts around means that used prices are low and there are plenty to choose from. Ford dealers not the best place to buy, plenty at car super-market sites. Specifications have improved over the years, aim for at least LX.

 ## Comfort ●●●○○

Refinement levels have improved and the Escort is a comfortable enough car for four adults. Passengers will feel plenty of bumps at low speeds. At least the seats are well shaped and snug. On the motorway, noise levels are acceptable. 1990 cars are crude; 1995 models are almost refined.

 ## Practicality ●●●○○

Reasonable-sized boot, useful split rear seats from LX model and very flexible small estate. An amazing amount of luggage can be piled inside.

 ## Driving ●●●○○

1990 Escort adequate, but not responsive, although it always feels safe. Needs power steering to be less hard work around town. From 1995 driver comfort is excellent and the new-style dashboard is clear to look at and easy to use. 1995 models have excellent steering, brakes and grip.

 ## Performance ●●●○○

The small engines offer small returns when it comes to performance, and that includes the diesel units, which remain noisy and slow. The 1.6 and 1.8 improve matters, offering decent acceleration and top speeds in excess of 100 mph, but most are economical and nothing more.

 ## Economy ●●●●○

Very good fuel economy overall, most models return late 30s to early 40s mpg. Unrefined diesel does not offer many advantages over petrol.

 ## Safety ●●●○○

Early Escorts quite poor, improved from 1992 with driver air bags a year later. ABS optional.

 ## Security ●●●○○

Engine immobiliser from 1992. Deadlock and alarm systems on certain models.

SUM UP

Which model?

Ideally the later the better. 1992 and then 1995 models are the only ones to buy. LX specification at least. Less popular saloon and three-door hatches can be surprisingly cheap. 1.6 engine is the pick of the range.

FOR Running costs. Practicality.

AGAINST Dull. Unrefined early models.

DOW RATING
●●●○○

Peugeot 306

1993 on

C H E C K P O I N T S

◆ Electrical problems, check windows, wipers, etc.

◆ High-mileage company cars ◆ Noisy engines ◆ Smoky diesels

306 profile

Peugeot set an impressive small-car standard with the very capable 306 back in 1993. There is a very pretty cabriolet, capacious estate, a dull but practical saloon and the very useful hatchback. There is also a large choice of engines.The 306 offers something for every driver and used-car buyer.

 Image ●●●●○

Although launched in 1993, the 306 is as good-looking as ever. It may primarily be bought as a hardworking diesel, saloon, or load-lugging estate, but the 306 is stylish and modern. It helps, of course, that there are some sexy cars in the range, from the head-turning cabriolet to the high-performance GTI-6.

 Running costs ●●●○○

Insurance starts at just group 4. Resale value is not bad, considering that this is primarily a high-volume fleet vehicle. The demand for used models remains strong. Servicing and parts slightly higher than average, though. From 1993 service intervals shifted from 6000 to 9000 miles on petrol models.

Reliability ●●●●○

Although Peugeot build quality is often criticised, it has improved dramatically, though, there are a number of electrical and minor mechanical problems.

 ### Value for money ●●●●○

A popular fleet car, there are increasing numbers of 306s on sale at Peugeot dealers and used-car supermarkets. Diesels, estates and the sporting versions are the most in demand. Prices for the saloons and most hatches are falling, and the standard specification is pretty comprehensive.

 ### Comfort ●●●●○

Less than brilliant interior. Nasty plastics, limited headroom in the front and the seats are sofa-soft. Great in your living room, not so good in a 306. It is saved by its excellent luxury-car ride.

 ### Practicality ●●●●○

Good interior storage space, especially the hugely practical hatchback and load-swallowing estate.

 ### Driving ●●●●●

Peugeot always manage to achieve the perfect ride/handling combination. Relaxing and refined 90 per cent of the time, and when you press on for the remaining ten per cent, the handling is truly remarkable. Whether estate, or GTI, the driver knows exactly how the 306 is behaving. Brilliant.

 ### Performance ●●●●○

The small 1.4 petrol engines are fine, offering good responses around town, but otherwise quite slow. The 1.8 litre is a good all-rounder, though, getting to 60 mph in ten seconds. The outstanding units are the very punchy yet frugal 1.9 turbo diesels and, of course, the six-speed 2.0 litre GTI, which gets to 60 mph in just over seven seconds.

 ### Economy ●●●●○

One thing a 306 can do is keep fuel bills down. The diesels average in the 40s and even the entry-level 1.4 petrol engine manages to get close.

 ### Safety ●●●●○

Driver air bags are standard on many models from 1994. Passenger air bags are mainly an option, along with side bags. ABS brakes are standard in many models.

 ### Security ●●●●○

There is an engine immobiliser, and on the sportier models an alarm. Unique-to-Peugeot music systems ought to deter thieves too. Highly effective deadlocks standard across the 306 range from 1998.

SUM UP

Which model?

Sturdy and practical 306 is one of the best small used cars you can buy. Turbo diesel combines remarkable economy with performance. Saloon is underrated, unpopular and therefore cheap. 1.6 is probably the best all-round engine.

FOR Driveability. Diesel engine.

AGAINST Interior.

DOW RATING
●●●●○

Renault Mégane
1996 on

CHECKPOINTS

◆ Noisy engines ◆ Oil leaks ◆ Starting problems
◆ Bodywork damage around boot and on bumpers ◆ Shabby interiors

Mégane profile

A family of small cars which includes a hatchback, saloon coupé and convertible, so there is something for everyone. Overall, the range is competent rather than outstanding, except for the mini MPV Scenic which deserves a five-star rating for being both original and highly flexible. Lots to choose from.

 Image ●●●●○

The Mégane's distinctive styling helps it to stand out from the small-car crowd; only the saloon manages to look a little dull. The same can't be said of the coupé, or convertible. Once again, the Scenic scores an impressive five stars because it is small, uniquely styled and every bit as practical as a full-size MPV.

 Running costs ●●●○○

Very reasonable servicing costs, one of the lowest in its class, and similar to the Clio. Insurance group starts at 4, and even the Scenic is a 5. Resale value for the majority of the range is strong indeed, especially the Scenic. Service intervals on the Mégane are usefully long at 10,000 miles for all petrol models.

Reliability

So far the Mégane has proved to be very reliable, with no major problems reported. Only build-quality niggles, relating to interior trim and minor electrical glitches.

 Value for money

Increasing numbers on the used-car market, although prices have stayed quite high. Decent level of standard equipment which includes power steering, driver air bag, electric sunroof (on all hatchbacks and the Classic saloon) and ABS brakes.

 Comfort

Plenty of interior space, whatever Mégane you choose. Scenic in particular is remarkably roomy. Soft seating spoils it a bit. Ride quality of the range is very good and makes it very comfortable for all passengers.

 Practicality

Big boot, lots of oddments space in hatch and saloon, while the Scenic has rear seats which slide forward to boost luggage room.

 Driving

A Renault built for comfort rather than handling pleasure. Good ride, but rolls on corners and best suited to motorway miles, when they are refined and quiet.

 Performance

There are lots of engine options. The 1.4 petrol isn't a bad unit, but the 1.6 is quick enough getting to 60 mph in less than twelve seconds, and also economical. The clutchless Easy is just that, a different but responsive manual/automatic. Good turbo diesel 1.9 is quick and frugal.

 Economy

Good overall fuel economy across the range. Most models offer over 40 mpg, but 1.6e has better consumption figures than 1.4e. Larger and heavier Scenic is slightly worse than hatches and saloons. Diesels offer middle 40s mpg figures.

 Safety

Driver air bag is standard, there are seatbelt pre-tensioners and optional passenger air bags, except for top model RXE Scenics where they are standard. ABS brakes are standard. Excellent performance in European crash tests. It can't be emphasized enough that the Mégane is one of the safest cars in its class and models introduced in 1996 managed to improve crash protection even further with better brakes and more air bags.

 Security

Only adequate locks, but there is an engine immobiliser which operates automatically, although an alarm is only standard on the convertible and coupé models.

SUM UP

Which model?

An excellent range. Versatile Scenic is the pick of the range, the 1.6e being the most economical version. Hatchback 1.6e good too, underrated and dull-looking saloon worth thinking about.

FOR Lots of choice. Scenic.

AGAINST Seats. Security.

DOW RATING
●●●●○

Rover 200/400
1989–95

CHECKPOINTS

♦ Oil leaks ♦ Noisy engines, especially diesels ♦ Shabby interior
♦ Broken headlights ♦ Clutch failure ♦ Parking dents

200 profile

The 200/400 was a Honda collaboration and proved to be very successful. The three- and five-door hatchbacks, along with the 400 saloon, were discontinued in 1995, although an estate, convertible and coupé model stayed in production until 1998. Easy to own and buy, the 200/400 range has become a reliable and sensible second-hand buy.

 Image

These models retain a certain old-world cred, mainly because they are old-fashioned. Possibly outdated cars for outdated buyers. The wedge-shape styling looks tired enough, but the hatchback and saloon still have a certain dignity. Image is middle-class and middle-aged and for many used-car buyers that can be a problem.

 Running costs

Running costs are not too bad and at least there are lots of second-hand parts around. 12,000-mile servicing intervals for the petrol cars is very generous. Insurance costs are average and start at group 7. Don't expect a high resale value, although demand for well-kept models will always be good.

Reliability ●●●●○

Average reliability for the older Rover products, which never really shook off the low build quality of previous generations. Engines are particularly good, provided they are well maintained. Important not to let small problems become bigger. Overall these Rovers can be relied upon although the electronic engine management system is costly to replace and in older examples can be more than the car is actually worth.

 Value for money ●●●○○

sale, but it is getting harder to an ex-company car examples. Often bought privately too, and these are the models to aim for, which will often be in pristine condition. Prices are very low.

 Comfort ●●●○○

nd stainless-steel door kick-plated is very well done. The seats are supportive and comfortable. Headroom is fine, but rear room in all models is tight. Reasonable ride in most models makes them not too bad.

 Practicality ●●●○○

estate is not that spacious. Decent ut interior accommodation is a let-down. Hard-working and reliable overall, though.

 Driving ●●●○○

er sits comfortably enough and itches fall conveniently to hand, but no model is a real driving pleasure. The coupé comes out best with decent handling and responses. Don't get a model without power steering if you do lots of town work, it is a pain to park.

  Performance ●●●●○

Most engine options are pretty sprightly, only the 218 diesel is slow. 16-valve engines best; 214 and 215 ideal all-rounders. 220 and 220 Turbo very fast.

  Economy ●●●●○

Fairly good mpg returns, 214 manages 40 mpg, performance models in low to mid-30s, diesels late 40s.

  Safety ●●●○○

Models got progressively better. Early ones had few features, but side impact bars from 1993, optional ABS too, although standard on sportier models. Later cars and coupés all had air bags and front seatbelt pre-tensioners.

  Security ●●●○○

Another instance where the range got better. Alarms from 1992 and an engine immobiliser from 1994.

SUM UP

Which model?

Becoming something of a budget-buy favourite. 214 or 216 make fine practical and economical buys, less popular 400 saloon likely to be cheaper too.

FOR Economy. Low prices.

AGAINST Tight interior. Lots of shabby ones around.

DOW RATING
●●●●○

Rover 200 **1995 on**

CHECKPOINTS

- ◆ Service history vital ◆ Water leaks through doors and sunroof
- ◆ Noisy high-mileage engines ◆ Brake judder ◆ Parking damage

200 profile

The Rover 200 is more supermini than small car, but it is a classy thing. Nicely styled, great to drive and well finished with a good choice of engines. However, both the three- and five-door is hampered by lack of room in the rear, which limits its practicality. Pricier than some rivals, it is the sophisticated rather than sensible choice.

 ### Image ●●●○○

This has been Rover's biggest problem for some time: what does it really stand for? Usually retired couples flying the flag in a chrome-grilled and wooden-dashed British built 200. That won't do. The 200 looks pretty, but does not stir much passion. Now if it had parent company BMW's blue and white badge on the front ...

 ### Running Costs ●●●○○

One of the cheapest Rovers to run. Although Rover servicing and parts are not known for their value, service intervals are placed a useful 12,000 miles apart, so should need just one service a year. Entry-level 211 offers group 3 insurance and resale value average, rather than outstanding.

Reliability ●●●●○

Has proved to be very reliable in service so far. No major problems; just the odd build-quality niggle and nothing more. Must be serviced properly, though.

Value for money ●●●○○

Lots to choose from now, and apart from a VW Golf, few other models manage to offer this level of quality. Specifications can be a bit mean. Power steering and a driver air bag are the 211 and 214 basics, but even the more expensive models don't add much more than a sunroof and remote central locking.

Comfort ●●●○○

The interior is very welcoming and smart. Rear legroom is restricted and makes it a pain for rear-seat passengers on long jaunts. The ride, though, is soft, but not too soft, and is very relaxing, both around town and on the motorway.

Practicality ●●●○○

Luggage room also is not overgenerous, and restricted rear legroom ultimately counts against this otherwise very useful car.

Driving ●●●●●

One problem for some drivers may be the low position of the steering column, even though it is height adjustable. The neat-looking dashboard has switches in odd places too. Otherwise this little car is very agile. Its steering is quick, and it clings to corners. Overall, refined rather than sporty.

Performance ●●●●○

Entry-level 1.1 is lively and refined. The bigger 1.4 and 1.6 16 valves are very quick, thanks to a slick gear shift. There are diesels; the most powerful turbocharged 220Sdi has almost sports car acceleration, whereas 200 VI petrol really does perform like a hot hatch should.

Economy ●●●○○

211 model offers 42 mpg, which is good. Cheapest of the lot to run is the 220D, which manages around 50 mpg.

Safety ●●●●○

Driver air bag is standard, passenger bag an extra, ABS brakes are only standard on the high-performance models. Centre three-point rear seatbelt is a nice idea, but a tight squeeze.

Security ●●●○○

There is an engine immobiliser which automatically sets itself, plus an anti-theft alarm. Door locks have to be regarded as a major weak spot. Independent tests have revealed that they are particularly easy to overcome.

SUM UP

Which model?

214 16-valve models offer the best combination of performance and very good economy. Diesels are good too, from the economy and performance angle, although don't match the overall refinement of the model. 200 VI is an underrated hot hatch.

FOR Engines. Styling. Handling.

AGAINST Cramped inside.

DOW RATING
●●●●○

Skoda Felicia 1995 on

CHECKPOINTS

♦ Bodywork parking damage ♦ Oil leaks ♦ Starting problems
♦ Minor electrical problems ♦ Central locking failure
♦ Worn steering and suspension

Felicia profile

A five-star budget five-door hatchback built by a company owned by VW. The estate version in particular represents fine value for money and is highly practical. They are cheap to buy and run and have a decent resale value. Bought nearly new, there is a comprehensive warranty package. What more could a private buyer want?

 Image ●●○○○

Despite a chintzy chrome grille the badge still says Skoda. For some snobby Brit buyers that is still a problem, despite the model's obvious talents and the wisdom of owning a car which is easy and cheap to run. The VW Group connection is helping.

 Running costs ●●●●●

The Felicia is very cost-effective, especially if bought at less than three years old because of its excellent warranty. Servicing is reasonable, insurance starts at just group 4 and premiums, especially for the more mature driver, are negligible.

Reliability ●●●●○

One of the best-built Skodas, thanks to owner VW's input. Apart from some minor electrical problems when first launched, it has proved to be a tremendously reliable buy.

Value for money ●●●●○

Skodas depreciate quickly in the first few years, and that makes the Felicia even more of a bargain. Low equipment levels on entry-level models. Power steering is only standard from the GLI. Then there is the balance of that fabulous warranty on any Felicias less than three years old.

Comfort ●●●○○

Roomy hatch and estate. Inside, the VW influence is obvious with quality trim and materials, which are tough yet attractive. The ride is a bit rough in town, there is some engine and road noise. Rear-seat passengers lack headroom.

Practicality ●●●○○

Practicality of the estate is astounding; the rear seats can even be removed to boost luggage room.

Driving ●●●●○

The driver sits in a comfortable enough seat, and is faced with usefully clear instruments and well-placed switches. The handling is secure and very safe. Around town, although the ride is jiggly, with power steering it is light and easy to manoeuvre.

Performance ●●●○○

Skoda's own 1.3 engines are adequate and less noisy than they used to be. Even

better is VW's 1.6 petrol engine with reasonable performance, getting to 60 mph in around thirteen seconds. Best all-rounder, though, is the 1.9 diesel, excellent low-speed power and economy.

Economy ●●●●○

Felicias are very fuel-frugal. All petrol engines are around 40 mpg, while the diesel is a healthy 50 mpg.

Safety ●●●●●

Only the entry-level 1.3 hatchback does not have an air bag, while SLXi has a passenger bag, plus ABS brakes. On the whole, for a budget car, levels of safety are perfectly adequate.

Security ●●●○○

Engine immobiliser is standard across the whole Felicia range, although locks are vulnerable. The badge seems to put most thieves off pinching a Skoda but it is worth installing some visual deterrents like steering locks so that an opportunist thief doesn't take advantage.

SUM UP

Which model?

The estate version – think of it as a larger hatchback – is hugely practical. 1.6 engine is the best option. Aim for highest specification, especially one fitted with power steering.

FOR Roomy. Quite refined. Good value.

AGAINST Image.

DOW RATING
●●●●○

Vauxhall Astra
1991–98

P860 OBH

CHECKPOINTS

♦ Rust indicates poor accident repair
♦ Smoking engines, especially diesels ♦ Clutch wear ♦ Sagging
suspension ♦ Electrical glitches, so try wipers, heater and windows

Astra profile

A perennially popular range of three- and five-door hatches, estate and saloon
which has proved to be reliable, cheap and very practical. The downside has
been that the Astra has become rather dull. For many used buyers that doesn't
matter, so long as it is economical and easy to own. The Astra is just that.

 Image ●●○○○

Never a pretty car, it is little more than
anonymous style-wise. Respected for its
ability to work hard, otherwise the Astra
blends into the traffic background. Even
the high-performance GSI never manages
to add any glamour to this lacklustre range.

 Running costs ●●●●○

As a small- to medium-sized petrol-engined
proposition, the Astra is a very cheap
vehicle to run. Service intervals are
9–10,000. Hard-used diesels demand more
attention at 5,000 miles. Insurance starts
at group 5 and premiums are very low.

Reliability ●●●●○

Astras last well, provided they are looked after, and often despite not being looked after. Although tough, the later 16-valve engines have been damaged by certain types of unleaded fuel.

 Value for money ●●●●○

Hundreds of thousands to choose from, which at least means there is no excuse for buying a bad one. Prices always on the low side and the arrival of the all-new model in 1998 means that used prices are even lower. Specifications have improved steadily over the years; revised range with large V on grille from August 1994.

 Comfort ●●●●○

All things considered, this basic car is nicely finished inside with a decent driving position and very supportive seats. Plenty of room in the back, for a change. The only let-down is a lack of refinement. You can hear road noise, and the ride is below the standard of most French rivals.

 Practicality ●●●●○

A good-sized boot, especially the estate and the saloon. Easy to load and most importantly, to live with.

 Driving ●●●○○

Not a lot of fun to drive, the Astra is merely adequate. For the majority of buyers that is fine. However, without power-steering the steering is very heavy around town.

 Performance ●●●○○

Smallest 1.4 (badged as a Hi Torq) is not very fast. However, more powerful 1.4 has similar good economy and reasonable

speed. 1.6 E-drive is also sluggish, so go for 1.6 16-valve for all-round ability. The 1.8 and 2.0 cars provide the hot hatchback fun.

 Economy ●●●●○

Very good fuel returns, with all but the performance versions managing over 40 mpg. Noisy diesel gets to 50 mpg, but the petrols are the best practical bet.

 Safety ●●●○○

Strong little cars which were gradually uprated. Some models had driver air bags as early as 1993. ABS, which is certainly worth having, is also fitted to some Astra models.

 Security ●●●○○

Only average protection on offer. Weak locks, although engine immobilisers from 1994 are optional.

SUM UP

Which model?

Five-door hatchbacks are very useful. Aim for the revised 1994 models with the higher-powered 1.4 or 1.6 engines. Saloons, badged as Belmonts, not so popular, and consequently much cheaper. Estates in particular are roomy and very useful.

FOR Cheap to buy and run. Decent amount of space.

AGAINST Not refined or very exciting.

DOW RATING
●●●○○

Volkswagen Golf
1984–91

CHECKPOINTS

♦ Minor rust only on tailgate and panel edges   ♦ Accident damage
♦ Altered mileage   ♦ Smoking engines   ♦ Water leaks

Golf profile

The Mark 2 Golf from the early 80s set the hatchback standard. No other car
came close in practical and quality terms, two factors which are important to
today's cost-conscious used car buyer. While most contemporary three- and
five-door hatches are falling apart, a 15-year-old Golf still has plenty to offer.
Booted version called the Jetta is often overlooked.

 Image   ●●●●●

Golf. You only have to say that one word for
everyone to understand what sort of car
you have bought into. It stands for classic
qualities and so far, timeless style. Many
also appreciate the fact that the Golf is
classless, yet the owner gets points for
their tasteful choice. GTI now legendary.
The Jetta is just a one-star car for style.

 Running costs   ●●●○○

Volkswagen parts are always more expensive than more ordinary hatchbacks, but
there is now a thriving national network of
specialists who can service and repair Golfs
for less. Lots of second-hand spares
around, too. VW have recently slashed the
cost of thousands of parts. Insurance
higher than average; starts at group 7.

Reliability ●●●●●

Old Golf is famously reliable. Careful looking after helps, but both major and minor components prove to be very durable. Rust on the vast majority of 80s survivors is still minor. Uncomplicated and tough mechanicals. Original build quality was brilliant.

 Value for money ●●●○○

Getting harder to find pristine Golfs, and prices for the best ones are never low, even though the model is getting on now. Pays for itself in the sense that good ones are always reliable, and there is still a healthy demand, so resale is easy.

 Comfort ●●●○○

In its day the Golf was regarded as spartan. There are not many standard creature comforts, but good seats, a bit tight in the rear and the ride may be a little firm for some. There is road noise too. Creaky by 90s standards, but still honest and snug enough for the budget, but quality-conscious, buyer.

 Practicality ●●●●○

Reasonable boot, although there are obstructions inside and a high loading lip. The Jetta's boot is absolutely huge. A vehicle that will work hard all day long.

 Driving ●●●●●

A safe and very sensible car to drive. The dashboard is old-fashioned, but very well laid out and logical with the radio where it should be, at eye level. In handling terms the Golf is secure on the road, and the GTIs in particular offer and deliver driving thrills. Some may find the mainly non-power-assisted steering on the heavy side.

 Performance ●●●●○

Not much in the way of performance until you get to the hot hatchback GTIs. Small-engined versions are best avoided, especially 1.0 and 1.3 litre. 1.6 and 1.8 are much better all round. Diesel is sluggish but frugal.

 Economy ●●●●○

Good overall mpg. 1.3 and 1.6 are both around 40 mpg, and diesel is over 50 mpg. Automatics and GTIs are the worst at early to mid-30s, but still impressive.

 Safety ●●●○○

Apart from build quality, no modern-day safety measures. Stands up well in an accident, though.

 Security ●○○○○

No factory-fitted protection, even on GTI models. Locks easy to overcome.

SUM UP

Which model?

1.6 or 1.8 Golf is a very good budget buy and worth five stars, but lost one because they are getting old now. Booted Jetta unfairly overlooked. Any Golf still sensible, after all these years.

FOR Build quality. Practicality. Reliability.

AGAINST Harder to find good ones. May feel dated.

DOW RATING
●●●●○

Volkswagen Golf
1992–98

CHECKPOINTS

♦ Poor accident repairs ♦ No rust ♦ Tyre wear at front
♦ Difficult gearbox/clutch at high miles ♦ Interior rattles on early examples ♦ Altered mileages

Golf profile

Third-generation Golf initially proved a disappointment, but has since gone on to establish itself as yet another no-worry used buy. The extended range now includes a five-door estate as well as the booted Vento, along with the familiar three- and five-door hatches. Proof that no one makes a mistake buying a used Golf.

 Image ●●●●○

This Golf did not quite have the visual impact of the previous generations, looking a bit soft and similar to a lot of other hatches. The badges, both VW and Golf, mean an awful lot. Still one of the smartest hatches to own and be seen in. GTI not as respected as previous generations.

 Running costs ●●●○○

10,000-mile service intervals are good, with the major garage visit coming at 20,000. Parts are always expensive, and running a Golf has to be regarded as an investment rather than a penalty. Insurance higher than the average hatch too.

Reliability ●●●●●

Although there have been some quality upsets in the early years, the Golf is very much back on track since then, with legendary levels of reliability. As ever, provided the Golf is well maintained, there won't be any worries.

 Value for money ●●●○○

Good Golfs are never cheap. Despite the launch of an all-new Golf in 1998, prices for the old model have not dropped signific-antly. Equipment levels are also basic. The saloon Vento version, though, is not in demand, but has all the Golf's qualities, but with a big boot and dull body. Worth thinking about.

 Comfort ●●●●○

Although the Mark 3 is different in character to previous Golfs, arguably a bit softer to drive, that has succeeded in making it much more comfortable. The seats are very good indeed and the interior is spacious.

 Practicality ●●●●○

Useful amounts of room, although the estate is only marginally bigger than the hatchback. Golf remains a stress-free, everyday, flexible and adaptable vehicle. The boot is usefully deep and folding the seats forward is easy, opening up masses of extra room.

 Driving ●●●●○

Softer set-up than previous Golfs means that the standard cars are quite pleasant with good grip and safe, precise behaviour on the road. GTI versions, though, not very sporty. If the steering is not power assisted, a Golf is very heavy to park.

 Performance ●●●○○

1.4 struggles with the heavy body, and the higher-power version of the 1.6 or a 1.8 is the best option. Diesels are slow, although the turbo version not so bad. 16-valve GTI gets a move on, 8-valve not worth the bother.

 Economy ●●●●○

Reasonable economy, diesels especially so. Slow 1.4 is the 42 mpg petrol; otherwise the majority of the engines hover around the mid-30s mpg.

 Safety ●●●○○

Good crash protection from this well-designed car, built in from the first models. Air bags from 1994, ABS brakes optional, tough standard on sportier versions.

 Security ●●●○○

Locks could have been better; fitted with an engine immobiliser from 1994.

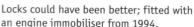

SUM UP

Which model?

Overall the range is excellent, but the engine size has to be chosen carefully as there are several options. The higher power 1.6 or 1.8 are the best, with the sprightly turbo diesel after them. Vento saloons should not be ignored.

FOR Comfortable. Reliable. Respect.

AGAINST Expensive.

DOW RATING
●●●●○

Citroen ZX 1991–98

CHECKPOINTS

- ◆ Easily dented bodywork ◆ Engines running roughly, poor starting
- ◆ Electrics can play up; test everything from wipers to windows
- ◆ Suspension worn

ZX profile

Citroen's version of the Peugeot 306, now replaced and looking a little dated. However, the ZX hatchbacks and estate models have proved to be cheap to buy, practical and economical. Performance and comfort levels are also very good, and only the slightly flimsy feel lets it down. Recommended.

 Image ●●●○○

All those stylish straight edges look more 80s than 90s now, so it won't win any beauty contests. ZX looks dull, but is actually quite fun to own and drive. Gets respect for being practical and that's it. Distinctly old-fashioned and middle-aged.

 Running costs ●●●○○

Earlier ZXs built up to 1994 only had 6,000-mile service intervals, after that 9,000. Insurance costs are reasonable, starting at just group 4. Depreciation is quite steep now, so likely to devalue quickly and not be so easy to resell.

Reliability

The only problem with the ZX has been a flimsy build quality which has shown up because so many have been used as mileage company fleet cars. Provided they are serviced there are no problems, but interiors and bodywork deteriorate when hard used.

 ## Value for money

The ZX has always proved popular with company fleets, which means there are always lots to choose from. Getting very cheap now, especially the early cars, but even the last 1998 models are tremendous value.

 ## Comfort

Difficult to argue with the way the ZX performs in this respect. Very roomy inside for such a compact car, with decent rear legroom. Seats could be too soft for some, but overall the ride is smooth and relaxing. Cheap interior fittings are the only let-down.

 ## Practicality

ZX in hatchback, and especially as an estate, proves to be very easy to live with; excellent load- and people-lugging abilities.

 ## Driving

ZX is a great car to drive. Good steering which is accurate and light. Good grip on corners and a fabulously smooth ride over the roughest road surfaces.

 ## Performance

The ZX has an excellent engine line-up which even makes the smallest 1.4 a lively performer; 1.6 is slightly more relaxed on the motorway, while 1.8, 1.9 and 2.0 litre cars are surprisingly quick. All diesels are quite swift too.

 ## Economy

The smaller petrol engines are all just under 40 mpg, while the diesels manage 50 mpg. Overall, economy is excellent right across the range, the only disappointing models are the bigger-engined petrol versions, the 1.9 and 2.0 manage just over 34 mpg. The high-performance 16V slips to 33 mpg.

 ## Safety

Good performance in crash tests. Side impact beams were introduced in 1993, seatbelt pre-tensioner system in 1994 and also a driver air bag.

 ## Security

Most ZX models got a keypad immobiliser (code had to be tapped in before it could be started) from 1994. Alarms also standard on some models, although breaking into a ZX is not difficult.

SUM UP

Which model?

Very cheap to buy and easy to own practical hatchback. 1.4 models are a good budget buy. 1994 on models have important safety upgrades. Estates are rightly sought-after. Ideal too as a diesel.

FOR Engines. Space. Economy.

AGAINST Style. Build quality.

DOW RATING

Rover 400 1995 on

CHECKPOINTS

♦ Oil leaks ♦ Electrics must be checked, wipers, windows, etc. ♦ Noisy engines at high miles ♦ Parking damage ♦ Exhaust prone to failure

400 profile

Compact and classy was Rover's idea for the range of 400 saloons and hatches and largely they have succeeded. Expensive when new, it is fast becoming a bargain used buy. It is very nice to drive, refined, smart and well put together. Promoted as a Ford Mondeo rival, the 400 is much smaller. As an upmarket alternative to a Ford Escort, it has to be taken seriously.

 Image ●●●○○

In the image game, Rover have started to get somewhere with the 400. There is something about the styling which suggests scaled-down Jaguar. It still has that frumpy grille, and Rover isn't regarded in the same class as Audi, or BMW. A cut above a Ford or Vauxhall, though. The 400 still has to try harder to impress.

 Running costs ●●●○○

Servicing is reasonable, reflecting the fact that Rover have aimed the 400 at fleet users with healthy 12,000-mile intervals between services. The 416 diesel is the cheapest model to run commercially. Insurance group starts at a high 9. The Rover 400 is becoming less attractive to re-sell so this makes it cheap to buy.

Reliability ●●●●○

So far the 400 has proved to be very reliable. It can take large mileages and heavy fleet use in its stride, provided it is properly serviced and has not been abused as a high-mileage company car.

 Value for money ●●●○○

So much better value used than it was new. Specification has been improved considerably over the years, but always well equipped with power steering, air bag, electric windows and roof for entry level. Lots around at supermarket used-car sites, pushing prices down even further.

 Comfort ●●●○○

Combine the standard equipment with the wood effect and chrome fittings, and the 400 is a pleasant place to be. Rear passengers, though, don't have much knee room. The ride is soft and very comfortable, soaking up the worst of inner city potholes and repaired motorway surfaces.

 Practicality ●●●○○

A good-sized boot on the 400. In service this model has proved to be a dependable and useful vehicle.

 Driving ●●●○○

The 400 is no sports saloon. Too much roll in corners, and the steering is just not sharp enough for the more enthusiastic driver to change direction rapidly. Otherwise it behaves itself, being refined and smooth. Easy to drive around town too.

 Performance ●●●●○

A good range of engines which have plenty of power and can be exploited at most speeds. The 1.4 is very eager and the 1.6 only marginally quicker. The 2.0, though, is the liveliest. The noisy diesels are also flexible and reasonably quick.

 Economy ●●●○○

Fuel consumption is good, averaging 40 mpg, except the 1.6 automatic and 2.0 litre, which only manage 32 mpg. Diesels get into the 50 mpgs.

 Safety ●●●●○

Driver air bags are standard, passenger ones are optional, but standard on higher specification models. ABS brakes are standard on all but the entry-level models. Saloons have a centre three-point seatbelt in the rear.

 Security ●●●●○

Remote central locking plus alarm and engine immobiliser are all standard fittings, and offer good levels of protection. Even the radio has security coding.

SUM UP

Which model?

As a used proposition, the 400 is very attractive. 414 is very good, 416 is the best compromise. Diesels are frugal if a little out of place in such a small, classy car. Saloons from 1996 are less in demand, so cheaper.

FOR Comfortable. Well equipped. Economical.

AGAINST Cramped rear.

DOW RATING
●●●●○

Citroen Xantia

1993 on

CHECKPOINTS

♦ Oil leaks ♦ Electrical problems, so ensure that electric windows and roofs work ♦ Complex hydraulic system; if neglected, affects steering, suspension and brakes ♦ Expensive to put right ♦ Service history essential

Xantia profile

The Xantia hatchback and estate compete against Mondeos and Vectras, but are refreshingly different thanks to their styling and the impressive ride quality of the Hydractive suspension. The interiors of the Xantia are comfortable and roomy too, plus there is a great range of dependable engines, including the legendary diesels. This is a much underrated used buy.

 Image ●●●○○

When everyone in the company car park has a Mondeo, or Vectra, the Xantia is more than likely to stand out from the crowd. Despite dating back to 1993, the design still looks very fresh, even though the interior is a bit of a disappointment. Something a bit different from the norm, like the owners.

 Running costs ●●●○○

Above average when something goes wrong, especially the electrics or suspension. Insurance groupings, though, start at 12 for hatches and 9 for the estates. Resale value overall is on the poor side; only the turbo diesels and some estates show a strong demand in later years.

Reliability ●●●○○

The Xantia has been around for quite some time and there are a number of faults, mainly related to the fact that it is used as a high-annual-mileage fleet car. Oil leaks, smoking high-mileage engines and electrical faults are the most common upsets.

 ## Value for money

Fleet market success means lots of used Xantias to choose from. Prices are low, as the car trade and buyers still remain sceptical about reliability, despite the success of this model. Good specifications on offer from LX model upwards.

 ## Comfort ●●●●●

The interior may not be the nicest to look at, but cruising down a motorway, or soaking up the potholes in town is all that matters. There is plenty of room and the suspension system does its stuff. A smooth, and ultimately relaxing, ride.

 ## Practicality

Plenty of room in both the hatch and the estate model.

 ## Driving

The Xantia manages to smooth out the roughest terrain with ease, and always feels safe and secure on the road. The Activia model's flat cornering suspension is unique. A Xantia is a car a driver will never tire of. A very relaxing way to travel and easy enough to operate around town, too.

Performance ●●●●○

There is a strong line of engines under the Xantia's bonnet. It starts to get lively from 1.8 upwards. The 2.0 is a strong unit and is very versatile as a turbo. The V6 is by far the smoothest and fastest and suits the Xantia's character perfectly. The responsive turbo diesels work the hardest and are best in the long-term.

 ## Economy ●●●●

V6 is by far the worst at 24 mpg. Petrol turbo 2.0 just manages 30 mpg, diesels, though, get 44 mpg and small petrol 1.6 to 1.8 up to 35 mpg.

 ## Safety ●●●●○

Early cars just three stars. From 1994 a driver air bag and seatbelt pre-tensioners were added, followed in 1998 by upgraded side impact protection and passenger bags, while ABS brakes are standard across the majority of the range.

 ## Security ●●●●○

Fiddly immobiliser keypad on early cars was replaced by a sensible key system. Recent models have an alarm and deadlocks.

SUM UP

Which model?

A Xantia always represents a risk, being less conventional than the obvious choices. However, a well-looked-after example ought to be worth considering if the price is right. At LX specification 1.8s, strong 2.0s or respected and frugal diesels.

FOR Roomy. Smooth ride. Diesels. Low prices.

AGAINST Reliability. Build-quality niggles.

DOW RATING
●●●●○

Ford Mondeo

1993 on

R36 UHM

CHECKPOINTS

♦ Interior trim quality on early cars is poor
♦ Electrical niggles, make sure all the controls work
♦ Watch out for altered mileages ♦ Clutch could be worn

Mondeo profile

A best-seller and deservedly so. Low running costs, practicality, comfort and, most surprisingly, keen driver's car. The Mondeo is proof that medium-priced, middle-market cars don't have to be dull, under-equipped and a bore to drive. Revised for the better in 1996. The Mondeo is a magnificent used buy.

Image   ●●●○○

The fact that it is a Ford does not help matters with hundreds of thousands in circulation, but the Mondeo gets more respect than previous mass-market Cortinas and Sierras. That's because it's a class leader, rather than being just a safe and reliable purchase.

Running costs   ●●●●○

The great thing about a car aimed at the fleet market is that servicing costs and procedures are straightforward, which makes the Mondeo cheap and easy to own. Less friendly is the fleet-car-sized depreciation, which affects the V6 and better equipped 2.0 versions worst of all.

Reliability ●●●●○

There have been relatively few problems with the Mondeo in service, mainly associated with high mileages and also minor electrical and trim defects. Overall, though, as reliable as a fleet car should be.

 ## Value for money ●●●●●

There are lots of Mondeos around and used prices are very low. Most are well equipped, especially post-1996 revised models, with all but the basic having a CD player and air-conditioning as standard.

 ## Comfort ●●●●○

Considering how much time users spend in a Mondeo, it is essential that everyone keeps comfy, and they do. Head and leg-room are fine and all but the most oversized rear-seat passengers have a decent amount of room. The ride is smooth and calming.

 ## Practicality ●●●●●

The Mondeo is very easy to live with. Plenty of cubby-hole space inside, with lots of luggage room and a useful flat loading bay on the estate.

 ## Driving ●●●●●

The Mondeo delivers a surprising amount of fun thanks to its excellent steering and balanced handling, which always feels safe and secure. The logical dashboard layout, nice controls and adjustable steering column all contribute to the rather wonderful driving experience that is the Mondeo.

 ## Performance ●●●●○

The entry-level 'economy' 1.6 engine may be frugal, but it is very slow. The 1.8 and 2.0 units are much more peppy, being smooth, but lack the real sparkle of the top of the range V6, which is a 130 mph flyer. The best compromise is probably the 1.8, although the diesels remain noisy, unrefined and slow.

 ## Economy ●●●●○

It depends which model you choose. They are economical, both the 1.6 and 1.8 return 36 mpg on average. Noisy turbo diesel gives 46 mpg.

 ## Safety ●●●●●

Very well built with driver air bag as standard equipment. ABS brakes on many models are also standard. A centre three-point seatbelt in the rear means five can travel in safety.

 ## Security ●●●●●

Mondeos built prior to 1996 are vulnerable. Five-star security from 1996 with the excellent deadlock system, plus an immobiliser and alarm, which makes the Mondeo very secure.

SUM UP

Which model?

An excellent range of cars. 1.8 is the best combination of economy and performance. V6 models are very fast, cheap and underrated.

FOR Styling. Handling. Running costs.

AGAINST Diesel engines. Lots around.

DOW RATING
●●●●●

Ford Sierra 1982–93

♦ Rust ♦ Noisy high-mileage engines
♦ Also worn suspension, steering and brakes on older models

Sierra profile

The Sierra took over where the old Cortina left off in terms of reliability and durability. An honest, lovable range of cars which includes roomy estates, the Sapphire-badged saloons and practical hatches. Still sought-after because the Sierra is well built, easy to work on and an attractive, cheap used buy.

 Image ●●●○○

Honest, working-class appeal. Only the high-performance Cosworths have any real presence; otherwise the Sierra and Sapphire simply get on with the job. Tough, usually a bit shabby, anonymous, a little dull-looking, but always reliable. Overall the image is low-rent, so not for snobs.

 Running costs ●●●●○

Last of the great DIY cars, if you are handy with a spanner. That also translates into cheap servicing and parts. Basically any competent mechanic can keep a Sierra going for ever. Lots of spares around. The only downside is fuel economy, which can be poor.

Reliability

Unburstable mechanicals in this car. Easy to maintain, so unlikely to break down, provided basic maintenance is part of the ownership routine. Old age and neglect will eventually kill the engine and see the onset of serious rust.

 ## Value for money

On the whole Sierras are very cheap, although the nicest cars from the last year of production, 1993, can still command high prices. Ghias and GLXs provide very good equipment levels. Examples with no history and lots of previous owners are best avoided.

 ## Comfort

Interiors wear very well indeed. Dated, but not uncomfortable driving position. Reasonable room in the back seat. But it's a hard ride and road noise isn't up to late 90s standards.

 ## Practicality

The Sierra is a real workhorse. Lots of room in the hatches and estates. Big boot on the Sapphire. Takes it all in its stride.

 ## Driving

Never exciting, just capable and, on the whole, safe. Harsh ride, noisy, but dependable. Heavy steering when not power assisted, but never out of its depth when being used around town. A good all-rounder.

 ## Performance

The 1.6 engine is not very powerful. The 1.8 engine is perky and the 2.0 litre all you will ever need, provided later post-1989 version is chosen. Diesels are truly awful: noisy, slow and unrefined. Cosworths are hugely fast, but it is hard to buy examples that haven't already been thrashed.

 ## Economy

Just over 30 mpg for the 1.6 and 1.8 models, pre-1989 2.0 very similar. Post-1989 2.0 litre gives 37 mpg, so choose carefully. The noisy diesel hardly seems worth it for just over 40 mpg.

 ## Safety

Good reputation for protecting occupants in a crash, especially later models. ABS optional and standard on some models.

 ## Security

Anti-theft alarms on some models from 1990; otherwise very easy to steal. Owners have to fit extra protection to be completely secure.

SUM UP

Which model?

Go for the latest model you can. Avoid anything pre-1988, which is likely to be quite tired and shabby by now. 2.0 litre engines offer the best performance/economy combination, although the 1.8 is also very good. Aim for good specifications too, like a Ghia, or GLX model. A five-star banger, but realistically a strong three-star rating for those on a budget.

FOR Cheap. Reliable. Easy to repair.

AGAINST Old, shabby Sierras.

DOW RATING

Nissan Primera
1990 on

CHECKPOINTS

- ◆ Rust means accident damage ◆ Oil leaks
- ◆ Adjusted mileage on ex-fleet cars ◆ Worn clutch and noisy suspension

Primera profile

The Nissan Primera saloon, hatchback and estate just about have it all: practicality, reliability and driveability. What the Primera does not have is any style. Completely revised in 1996, it looks like the old one, and unfortunately many buyers still overlook the British-built model's many abilities. This is one of the most underrated family cars on sale today, and a great used buy.

 Image

Unfortunately, Nissan have missed a huge opportunity with the Primera which has not made much impression on anyone, and parked in the street blends into the background. Without the distinctive styling of a VW Passat, or Ford Mondeo, the Primera struggles in the style stakes.

 Running costs

Nissan have aimed the Primera squarely at the fleet market, and that means servicing costs at 9,000- and 18,000-miles are reasonable. Insurance groupings start at 8. Resale values are typically average, like most fleet cars. Easy for any garage to service which keeps costs down.

Reliability

No worries for a company car like this, which can easily rack up a six-figure mileage over a few years. Great build quality means this is a model that will last.

 Value for money

Company-car fleet market success means there are lots around, especially nearly new examples. Always well packaged, the latest models all have ABS brakes, driver air bag and deadlocks. Plus there may be the balance of the three-year new car warranty.

 Comfort

The interior may be very well built, but it is dull. At least there is plenty of room in the front and rear. Legroom is fine in the back, but headroom can feel limited. The ride overall is fine for passengers.

 Practicality

The boot is big, hatchbacks and saloons are roomy and useful. However, the estate has its limitations, despite clever 12-volt power point and a tray for muddy boots on the most recent versions.

 Driving

For the driver who cares beyond the clearly laid-out fascia and despite a seat which can be a pain to adjust correctly, is a car which handles superbly. Plenty of grip, minimal body roll and secure behaviour mean that it is possible to push the Primera hard without ever losing control. Very sporty.

 Performance

The smallest 1.6 engines are eager. However, the 2.0 litre works best with the Primera's sports car handling, being smooth and responsive. The even more powerful GT proves to be the motorway mile-muncher, while the diesel is efficient, but unremarkable.

 Economy

Fuel consumption for the majority of the range is good. 40 mpg for the 1.6 and diesel, otherwise the average is mid-30s mpg.

 Safety

The significant dates are 1993 when side impact protection was fitted, and a year later when driver air bags were made standard. ABS brakes are present on all post-1996 models. Seatbelt pre-tensioners are also part of the package.

 Security

Just an engine immobiliser on the early models, which won't rate higher than three stars. However, from 1996 standard dead-locks were fitted across the range, which are the best way of preventing a break-in. Not all models have alarms.

SUM UP

Which model?

The later the model, the better; big improvements from 1996. Also 1994 security and safety upgrades are important. The early version now a great budget buy. 1.6 for economy; 2.0 for added performance. You choose.

FOR Engines. Build quality. Handling.

AGAINST Styling. Nissan badge.

DOW RATING
●●●●○

Rover 600 1993 on

CHECKPOINTS

♦ Electrical problems, check windows and wipers ♦ Parking damage on bumpers and mirrors ♦ Gearbox problems ♦ Shabby or damaged interiors

600 profile

This has been Rover's version of a Honda Accord, which was replaced by the new 75. Although it has shown promise, the single saloon body style, cramped interior and build-quality shortfalls have been a let-down for new buyers. Now, though, used buyers can get their hands on this smart-looking car very cheaply.

 Image ●●●○○

The 600 sums up the Rover's identity problem. It looks the executive-car part, but has never been completely convincing. There may be bits of chrome, but there is still a lot of Honda. It won't impress the neighbours for long, especially if they drive a proper executive in the shape of an Audi, or BMW. Classier than any Ford or Vauxhall though.

 Running costs ●●●○○

Not a particularly cheap executive car to run, with service inspections every 6,000 miles, although dealer charges are containable. Insurance starts at group 10. Depreciation quite steep and getting steeper, so not a used buy to resell quickly. This is a model to keep for the long term. For the class of car fuel economy is good and that helps to keep overall costs down.

Reliability

So far the 600 has stood up well to high-mileage fleet use, although it must be serviced to schedule. A few build-quality and minor electrical upsets have been reported. Certainly paintwork could have been better on early cars.

 ### Value for money

Never a cheap option when new, it becomes something of a bargain now, especially as it has been replaced. Increasing numbers at supermarket sites and being sold cheaply by Rover dealers.

 ### Comfort

Lots of chrome, stainless steel and wood creates a nice interior ambience. No problems for the two people up front with large and very comfy seats. Anyone sitting behind has a much more cramped time of it. Although the 600 is meant to be tuned for comfort rather than performance, the firm ride can upset those inside.

 ### Practicality

Big boot, but the cramped interior lets the 600 down. Does not feel very versatile, especially as there is no hatchback option.

 ### Driving

The driver might like the look of the dashboard, but some of the Honda switches look out of place. The 600 is hardly dynamic, when the executive-class car demands it, being merely safe and secure. Nothing to get very excited about.

 ### Performance

Smallest 1.8 has proved to be a very accomplished performer. A low power output, but eager to accelerate and performance is similar for both the 2.0 and 2.3 litre models. 620ti turbo, though, is very quick. The diesel engine is very flexible, good value, but noisy.

 ### Economy

The majority of petrol motors just manage 30 mpg, although the diesels get close to 50 mpg and the 1.8 a creditable 41 mpg.

 ### Safety

Not impressive in independent crash tests. ABS brakes were added to most models by 1996. Driver air bags were added in 1994, and air bags are also optional for the passenger.

 ### Security

Engine immobiliser and alarm upgraded in 1994 and 1996. Visible vehicle identification numbers are a deterrent, but the Rover 600 is still vulnerable to break-ins. The door locks could certainly be so much better.

SUM UP

Which model?

The 618 is a great all-rounder offering performance and economy, and has many improvements because it was launched in 1996. Otherwise the 620 is a relaxed motorway car. Top specifications like SLI and GSI are better value.

FOR Classy. Becoming affordable.

AGAINST Cramped. Poor image.

DOW RATING

Vauxhall Cavalier
1988–95

CHECKPOINTS

♦ Oil leaks ♦ Noisy gears which are difficult to engage ♦ Smoking and worn engines ♦ Lots of previous owners ♦ Incorrect mileage

Cavalier profile

The Cavalier has a lot going for it. What made it a sound purchase in the late 80s still holds true today. Cavaliers are cheap and economical to own. Even though finding nice examples is getting harder, it is worth making the effort if you want a safe and predictable saloon, or a hatchback that won't let you down.

 Image ●●○○○

Not the sort of car that is going to stir any strong emotions. The Cavalier is an odd, but very well-established name which stands for reliability and not much else, apart from dullness. There is nothing very cavalier about the Cavalier; that is probably its appeal.

 Running costs ●●●●○

Millions of Cavalier owners can't be wrong: running a Cavalier cost-effectively is easy. Lots of cheap parts around and easy DIY, or local garage servicing every 9,000 miles. Insurance premiums are low too. When it comes to this class of family car, nothing else is as cheap to buy or run.

Reliability ●●●●○

As the Cavalier gets older, owners neglect them which is when the trouble starts; otherwise, a well-proven high-miler. Regular servicing is essential for long life. Overall, though, a painless vehicle to own.

 Value for money ●●●●○

90s Cavaliers got progressively better equipped, and it is best to stick with cars from this decade in terms of condition, as older models look very shabby. Now very cheap, but it pays to choose carefully. Arguably one of the very best budget buys.

 Comfort ●●●○○

The Cavalier was designed for drivers who spend hours behind the wheel, and it is still a comfortable place to be after all these years. Limited rear room, but not a tight squeeze. There is a reasonable ride, and those after lots of creature comforts should buy a CDX model.

 Practicality ●●●○○

Good-sized boot. Hatchback, in the absence of an estate, gets the load-lugging vote. Tough and durable.

 Driving ●●●○○

Predictability is what the Cavalier is all about. No real driving pleasure as such, just a competent car which is fine on the motorway and behaves itself around town, although a model with power steering would be a good idea. Not remotely sporty, even the one with a GSI badge on the back.

 Performance ●●●●○

Noisy, but honest and quite powerful engines, especially the 2.0 litre. The cheap V6 is a real performance bargain and the 1.7 turbo diesel is very refined. Sluggish and small 1.4 engine is best avoided.

 Economy ●●●●○

Excellent overall economy across the range. 1.6s return over 40 mpg, diesels 47 to 49 mpg. 2.0 litre 36 mpg. Even the high-performance V6 engine manages a creditable 31.3 mpg and the rare four-wheel-drive turbo stays above 30 mpg, but only just.

 Safety ●●●○○

The Cavalier caught up quickly in safety terms; side impact bars in 1992, followed by driver air bag in 1993 and ABS on some models in 1994.

 Security ●●●●○

Deadlocks from 1992 are excellent. VIN (vehicle identification) numbers on front and rear screens by 1994, engine immobiliser on certain models.

SUM UP

Which model?

A great bargain buy. 1.8 is the best all-round engine. The 2.0 engine is slightly quicker, but with similar economy and more relaxed on the motorway. Hatches in demand more than saloons.

FOR Reliable. Economical. Lots to choose from.

AGAINST Hard ride. Booming engines. Dull drive.

DOW RATING
●●●○○

Vauxhall Vectra
1991 on

CHECKPOINTS

- ◆ Accident and parking damage ◆ Boot area damage ◆ Gearbox
- ◆ Engine running erratically ◆ Adjusted mileage
- ◆ Worn high-mileage cars ◆ So-so steering ◆ Suspension is sloppy

Vectra profile

For family transportation and business travel, it is hard to think of a better companion than the Vectra. Easy to drive, great at motorway speeds, a roomy, solid and reliable range of hatchbacks, saloons and estates. Not as charismatic as some in this class, such as the Ford Mondeo, but it offers economy and long-term low running costs. A good used car which is getting cheaper all the time.

 ### Image   ●●●○○

The Vectra lacks the sparkle which lifts it above being anything more than a hard-working fleet car. Hardly stylish to look at, it manages to merge into the background. For the majority of owners who just want to get on with the business of going about their business, that's fine. There are lots around so buyers think it's a safe bet.

 ### Running costs   ●●●●○

Fleet users want containable costs which is what everyone gets. Fixed-priced servicing at dealers every 10,000 miles, cheap parts and over 500 dealers help. Group 6 insurance is also a starting point. Depreciation is heavy as this is a mass-market car, so never worth selling in the short-term.

Reliability ●●●○○

No really serious problems reported so far, apart from some electrical glitches. Only neglect and very high mileages cause noticeable wear and tear. However, some owners have pointed out that the quality of the paintwork and interior trim could be better. If the owner has skipped services it could cause problems.

 Value for money ●●●●○

Plenty of Vectras on sale and that number is increasing all the time. Huge choice of models with good basic specifications. Driver air bag, ABS brakes, power steering and deadlocks are standard right across the range in the last few years.

 Comfort ●●●●●

Great news, the Vectra is brilliantly comfortable. Not only is the driver well positioned in a well-supported and high seat, rear head- and legroom is among the best in this class. Swing-out cup holders are something you would expect, although the excellent ride is a nice surprise.

 Practicality ●●●●○

There are plenty of storage cubby holes and nice touches, like an easy to operate split-fold rear seat and decent-sized boot, although the estate is not as big as others in this class.

 Driving ●●●○○

If the Vectra is used as the maker intended, to rack up motorway miles and normal urban errands, the supple ride will be comfortable enough. Anything more reveals that the Vectra is no sports car. Only the four-star GSI has the suspension modifications for the more enthusiastic driver.

 Performance ●●●●○

The 1.6 is economical, but underpowered. The 16-valve version and the 1.8 are much more sprightly. Gearboxes are quite smooth and the 2.0-litre diesel matches the petrol versions for acceleration. The 2.5 V6 is probably the best of its type and is fast too.

 Economy ●●●○○

Fuel consumption is impressive at 37 mpg for the 1.6, but most mainstream models return around 34 mpg.

 Safety ●●●●○

Standard driver air bag and ABS brakes are good features. Third three-point rear belt from LS upwards.

 Security ●●●●○

Deadlocks and engine immobiliser are standard. On GLS models, anti-theft alarms are fitted.

SUM UP

Which model?

1.8 Vectras with at least LS specification. Saloons are downvalued so cheaper, and worth considering. V6 can be very cheap and offers big-car comfort and performance.

FOR Engines. Driving position. Running costs.

AGAINST Ordinary to drive. Ordinary looks.

DOW RATING
●●●●○

Volvo 440/460
1988–97

CHECKPOINTS

♦ Minor rust ♦ Overheating engines ♦ Gearboxes difficult to use
♦ Smoky engines ♦ Service history essential
♦ Electrical problems, so try all the gadgets

400 profile

The 440 hatchback has always disappointed, even though it does have some merits in that it is practical and can be reliable, if looked after. 440 plus a boot equals the 460, which was an improvement on the 440. Better quality and a more coherent model. Both are safe, well-equipped and surprisingly cost-effective used buys.

 Image ●●●○○

Safe. If the name Volvo means anything it is that one word. Although modern Volvos are getting sexy, that is not something the 400 series can be accused of. Dull, sensible, but certainly better-looking after a 1993 facelift. Other motorists won't envy a 400, but they will respect it.

 Running costs ●●●○○

Renault engines ought to be a clue that there are lots of second-hand parts about, so there is no reason to break the bank with this Volvo. Potentially it can be run on a tight budget. Insurance starts at just group 5 proof that running a Volvo need not be an expensive proposition.

Reliability ●●●○○

Not great initially. Harmed Volvo's reputation no end, mainly due to French engines and Dutch build quality. Electrics, engines and clutches weak, but once sorted it soldiers on. Most, and certainly those built since 1993, are much improved.

Value for money ●●●○○

Important to shop around. Well cared for private-owner examples are the best. Multi-owner tatty examples are to be avoided. The 460 saloon model in particular is overlooked, underrated and often cheap. Equipment levels can be on the spartan side.

Comfort ●●●○○

The 440 never really feels like a quality car. A fair amount of room inside, even in the back. Interior fittings are cheap. At least the dashboard layout is good and the ride is quite smooth and comfortable. The 460 saloon is a lot more refined and probably worth an extra star.

Practicality ●●●○○

Big boots on both models, plus spacious interiors, make the 400s potentially useful, provided there are no reliability doubts.

Driving ●●●○○

A big surprise is that the 400s handle and stop very well. They could almost be described as agile. The big disappointment has always been the engines, which lack any excitement.

Performance ●●●○○

The turbo version has proved quick, but not the most practical, or durable model. All the other units feel desperately slow and very dull, even though performance is actually reasonable. The 2.0 is most relaxing, but the smallest 1.6 is capable enough.

Economy ●●●○○

Not bad; all engines return mid-30s mpg, while the noisy, but otherwise frugal, diesel manages 46 mpg.

Safety ●●●●○

You just automatically feel safe in a Volvo, even though active items were only fitted from 1993 in the shape of a driver air bag, side impact protection and seatbelt pretensioners.

Security ●●○○○

Despite Volvo's reputation for safety they are not so hot for security, especially on earlier examples. Engine immobilisers were fitted eventually and anti-theft alarms on top models, but they are still an easy target for thieves.

SUM UP

Which model?

460 is the most accomplished and Volvo-like of the range. 440 has the practicality edge, but the 460 is also likely to be slightly cheaper. Aim for the later and prettier post-1993 model with 1.8 or 2.0 power.

FOR Big boot. Safe. Practical.

AGAINST Unreliable for a Volvo. Poor image.

DOW RATING
●●●○○

Toyota Carina E
1992–97

CHECKPOINTS

◆ Service history ◆ Noisy engines ◆ Stone chips
◆ Mileage altered ◆ Ex-taxis

Carina profile

A car that Britain can be proud of. Built over here and tuned for European tastes (hence the E), the Carina E hatchbacks, saloons and estates are the ideal used cars. The only trouble is that reliable things tend to be dull as well. The Carina is bland, but that is better than regular exciting breakdowns. Very dependable.

 Image   ●●○○○

The poor old Carina hasn't really got one and few people realise that it is built in Britain. Not much credibility when it comes to styling. Carina does not mean much except yet another weirdly named, boring yet reliable, Japanese car. Canny used buyers, though, are laughing.

 Running costs   ●●●●○

Toyota parts and servicing are always at the high end of the scale. However, the fleet car market and British location have made Carina E parts cheaper to obtain. A Toyota that can be run on a tight budget. Insurance starts at group 8, although premiums tend to be reasonable.

Reliability ●●●●●

Although the Carina is reported for breakdowns more often than other Toyotas, that is explained by fleet-car use and huge fleet-car mileages. On the whole, faultless. Beware ex-taxis, though. A prime target to have its high mileage 'reduced'.

Value for money ●●●●○

The arrival of the Carina replacement called the Avensis in 1998 has hit Carina prices hard. Lots are coming off company fleets, so there is a huge choice and most have comprehensive specifications. Buyers get a lot of car for their money.

Comfort ●●●●○

There is no shortage of room inside a Carina. In the front and back, passengers can really stretch out. Never mind the plastic interior, its big-car feel puts the Carina in the executive class. Overall, very relaxing.

Practicality ●●●●○

The sheer size of the car means that it swallows people and luggage easily; ideal for every family.

Driving ●●●○○

Nothing to get excited about, just incident-free progress from A to B, which is what a family car should do. Having said that, handling is competent and safe, no nasty surprises, just a sensible car going about its business without being sporty.

Performance ●●●●○

A good range of engines. Smallest 1.6 and 1.8 have similar economy and performance figures, but the larger unit is less stressed.

2.0l version is usefully quick and GTI 2.0 versions are not much faster. The diesel is too slow; the turbo diesel is tough and provides better acceleration.

Economy ●●●●○

1.6 lean-burn engine is the really economical one, 42 mpg overall, just like the turbo diesel and 1.8. The sluggish diesel manages 48 mpg.

Safety ●●●○○

A safety review in 1994 added a driver air bag and optional ABS; seatbelt pre-tensioners followed a year later. A passenger air bag was added from March 1996.

Security ●●●○○

Average protection with an alarm and engine immobiliser on some models from 1995, and remote alarm in 1996. Despite being a popular choice for company fleets these are quite easy to steal. It is essential to fit some sort of visual deterrent such as a steering lock.

SUM UP

Which model?

Hatchbacks are very roomy and very practical. The 1.8 combines economy with more relaxed progress than the 1.6. 2.0 petrol is surprisingly swift. Estate is very underrated.

FOR Roomy. Refined. Well equipped. Reliable.

AGAINST Dull to look at and drive.

DOW RATING
●●●●○

Citroen Synergie/ Fiat Ulyssee/ Peugeot 806   1995 on

CHECKPOINTS

♦ Tyre wear   ♦ Suspension damage   ♦ Interior trim damage

Synergie profile

The Citroen Synergie came about as the result of cooperation between Fiat (the Ulyssee) and Peugeot (the 806). Same people movers, but different badges. Up against the class-leading VW Sharan and Ford Galaxy, the Synergie is really an also-ran. Competent rather than outstanding, although there are a few neat touches which boost interior flexibility.

 Image   ●●●○○

While most people movers try to look less like a commercial vehicle with windows, the Synergie seems to have been deliberately designed to be dull and boxy. Up against the Ford and VW on the school run it looks uninspiring. It does the people-moving job, but does not have a distinctive Citroen, Fiat or Peugeot character.

 Running costs   ●●●○○

Big-car running costs, even though it looks like a van. Much like most other people movers, in fact, although diesel versions become cheaper overall and more desirable when used. Insurance hovers around groups 10 to 12. Resale values are no better than average. Parking damage to panels can prove costly.

Reliability ●●●○○

No major problems reported so far, just the usual owner-inflicted damage and failures. There are some minor build-quality and electrical niggles, and they do feel flimsier than the Ford Galaxy or the VW Sharan.

 ## Value for money ●●●○○

Not the most desirable people mover, although a Peugeot-badged diesel or Citroen command highest used prices. When it comes to specifications, the Synergie seems to offer the most kit for the least money. The SX model in particular has air-conditioning, sunroof and rear electric windows, which will help resale prospects no end.

 ## Comfort ●●●○○

It feels roomy up front, thanks to the dashboard-mounted gear lever and right hand side handbrake. In certain tight parking situations the rear sliding doors help. Not a lot of rear headroom, although ride quality is perfectly acceptable.

 ## Practicality ●●●○○

Access to the last row of seats is not that easy. Potential eight-seater if the rear seats are replaced by a bench. No room for their luggage, though. Twin rear sliding doors are convenient. Overall these models are easy to live with when it comes to transporting lots of people, or fewer people and their luggage.

 ## Driving ●●●○○

The driving position is high and there is a long sloping nose. There isn't much in the way of driving enjoyment, especially when compared to the superior Ford and VW offerings. Otherwise it handles like a car.

 ## Performance ●●●○○

Just the two engines, a 2.0 litre petrol and 1.9 turbo diesel. Both are adequate, but the Synergie is heavy and slow.

 ## Economy ●●●○○

Oddly, there are mpg variations between all three versions with the Peugeot coming out best at 36.3 mpg for the diesel and 29.3 mpg for the petrol.

 ## Safety ●●●○○

Driver and passenger air bags on the Peugeot, just the driver on the Fiat and Citroen. Most higher-spec models also have ABS brakes.

 ## Security ●●●○○

Immobiliser is standard on all models, and on some models there are also optional alarm systems.

SUM UP

Which model?

Careful comparing of the specification puts the Citroen Synergie first. However, the Peugeot is the most economical and has the best reputation for making family diesels. Fiat, though, could turn out to be the cheapest used buy. The best advice is to shop around.

FOR Comfortable. Easy to use and park.

AGAINST Dull. Not that roomy.

DOW RATING
●●●○○

Ford Galaxy/ Volkswagen Sharan/ SEAT Alhambra   1995 on

CHECKPOINTS

♦ Minor electrical faults, so try all the gadgets   ♦ Check for interior damage
♦ Ex-taxis ♦ Mileage altered

Galaxy profile

The Galaxy may look more familiar than most people movers, and that is because VW have their own Sharan version and SEAT have the Alhambra. The Galaxy is very practical, with a good range of engines, being easier to own and drive than many other people movers. Hugely comfortable, and basically a simple but effective package.

 Image   ●●●●○

The Galaxy is Britain's favourite people mover, and that is no surprise given how handsome the styling is. The Ford badge also helps to make it a classless package. A VW badge manages to take the whole package upmarket and the SEAT, one step down. The Galaxy is perfectly in the middle.

 Running costs   ●●●●○

Low Ford repair bill means insurance starts at a very friendly group 10. Easy to service and 10,000-mile service interval is good. Resale value is not as strong as the VW Sharan, but not too bad compared with many people movers. Arguably one of the cheapest people movers to buy and run.

Reliability ●●●○○

So far reliability has been very good with the Galaxy, suffering damage only at the hands of owners and electrical glitches.

Value for money ●●●●○

Lots of used Galaxies around at car supermarkets and Ford dealers, so prices are low. The Sharan is mostly at VW franchises and is expensive. SEATs are somewhere in the middle, often with more equipment and at a lower price.

Comfort ●●●●●

The ride is firm, especially around town, but not uncomfortable and it comes into its own on longer motorway hauls. Driver gets a commanding view. Great accommodation for all passengers.

Practicality ●●●●●

The seven-seat option makes sense, and any of the rear five seats can be removed, which makes it nicely versatile. As with any people mover, though, a full complement of passengers limits luggage space.

Driving ●●●●●

The Galaxy is a big vehicle, but it certainly does not feel like one on the move. This is as easy to drive as a Mondeo both in town and on the open road, with a responsive power-steering system and light gear change. The firm suspension means it always feels stable when cornering, with little body roll, and on long journeys it is never less than relaxing.

Performance ●●●●○

The 2.0 litre is underpowered and struggles with that big body, but the unique-to-Ford

2.3 is a good acceleration/economy compromise. The smooth V6 fitted to the VW and Ford offers similar performance, but economy is poor. The diesels are adequate rather than exciting performers.

Economy ●●●○○

Fuel consumption not a V6 strong point just over 20 mpg, but the diesel is better with just over 40 mpg. Ford's 2.3 manages 28 mpg, the same as the 2.0.

Safety ●●●●○

Driver air bag is standard on Ford and VW, but twin air bags on SEAT. ABS brakes on some models. Probably the safest people mover on sale.

Security ●●●●○

Engine immobilisers across the ranges, from 1997 deadlocks on doors which are the best protection against break-ins. Alarms on many models.

SUM UP

Which model?

Huge numbers of Galaxies on sale means a larger choice and lower prices. The SEAT is fabulous value, usually with a very comprehensive specification and low prices, but few around. The VW has snob appeal because of the prestigious badge.

FOR Comfort. Room. Engine options.

AGAINST Luggage room when loaded.

DOW RATING
●●●●●

Renault Espace
1991 on

REN 130

CHECKPOINTS

♦ Electrical problems   ♦ Damaged interior
♦ Parking-damaged exterior   ♦ Poor gear change

Espace profile

The first and best European people mover, the Espace carries on its class-leading tradition, remaining the best upmarket people mover you can buy new or used. Comfortable, refined and practical, Renault widened the appeal of the range by adding the larger Grand Espace with a fully revised model in 1997.

 ### Image   ● ● ● ● ●

Regarded as the original and best people mover. Renault have not just relied on the Espace name, they have always updated the model, which still looks fresh and futuristic. In image terms, there is no people mover with a higher credibility rating than the Espace. It never looks out of place and seemingly will never go out of favour.

 ### Running costs   ● ● ● ○ ○

The Espace is an overgrown estate car and servicing costs are in that region, about the same as most executive models. Parts can be pricey. Insurance group starts at a reasonable 11, and resale value is among the best. Only the pointless V6 depreciates fast. Not the people mover for families on tight budgets.

Reliability ●●●○○

Minor quality hiccups have affected the Espace over the years, but it seems better built than ever now. Problems only with heavy use and neglect. Older Espaces do look their age.

Value for money ●●●○○

Never a huge number of used models on sale, and the best ones are sought-after and pricey. Some models are under-equipped. Even old and shabby Espaces can be premium-priced. Shop carefully.

Comfort ●●●●●

The Espace has all sorts of clever touches, which boost luggage and oddments space. On the 1997 models, the fabric-trimmed dashboard even houses a briefcase box, plus individual ventilation controls for those in the front. Well designed and roomy.

Practicality ●●●●●

The Espace is always more capacious than its early rivals. The latest, stretched, Grand Espace seats seven easily, and, most importantly, that includes their luggage.

Driving ●●●●○

The Espace has always been easy to operate, despite an upright driving position and the pedals being offset. The steering is light and precise with typical French softness to the suspension, which means body roll on corners and a slightly bouncy ride. On the move it is refined, giving a decent ride, and is very easy to park.

Performance ●●●○○

2.0 litre models are underpowered and the 2.2 petrol unit is only slightly better. The turbo diesel has a similar power output, but proves to be much more usable, with good acceleration if noisy. The V6 engine is fast, but not frugal.

Economy ●●●○○

Just over middle 20s mpg for the 2.0 petrol, and just over middle 30s for the diesel. V6 on later models is barely 20 mpg.

Safety ●●●●○

Driver air bag from 1995, and passenger air bags are now standard across the range, as are ABS brakes from 1997. If you want a safe people carrier then the later Espace is the one to go for and rates a full five stars in this respect. Probably the safest car in its class.

Security ●●●○○

Remote locking, engine immobiliser and an alarm are all standard throughout the range from 1997, previously only fitted to RXE models.

SUM UP

Which model?

1995 models were thoroughly revised with extra safety features, so worth finding. Diesels are always more sought-after and therefore more pricey. The V6 is always cheap, but there is a price to pay when it comes to servicing and economy. 2.0 is the best bargain.

FOR Space. Style. Refinement.

AGAINST Pricey.

DOW RATING
●●●●○

Land Rover Discovery

1989 on

CHECKPOINTS

♦ Oil leaks ♦ Gearbox problems ♦ Worn clutches ♦ Smoking diesel
engine ♦ Damaged interior ♦ Worn steering and suspension

Discovery profile

For on-road refinement and off-road ability, the three- and five-door Discovery
has the perfect combination of these two virtues. It has everything Land Rover
needs to succeed in the marketplace between the toy off-roaders and luxury
Range Rovers. Despite unreliability, the Discovery has never gone out of
fashion. Brand-new and much revised 1998 model better in every respect.

Image   ♦♦♦♦♦

No other off-roader has the reputation of
the Discovery when it comes to going off-
road, or posing on the road. Whatever the
quality and reliability troubles, customers
remain loyal, and the Discovery's reputation
remains intact. New 1998 model looks like
the old one, because the design is a classic.

Running costs   ♦♦♦○○

Diesel Discoveries have always proved much
more popular than the petrol V8. Servicing
and parts are not cheap, but 12,000-mile
service intervals spread the cost and
insurance starts at a reasonable group 11.
Depreciation on the latest 1998 diesel Tdi
in particular will be very low.

Reliability ●●○○○

Discoveries have been notoriously unreliable. 1998 models are much improved, but all previous models need to be checked carefully.

Value for money ●●●○○

The arrival of the all-new Discovery has started to make older versions cheaper. The unpopular three-door model remains the bargain of the range; V8s are, too, if you can afford the petrol.

Comfort ●●●●○

The interior always feels roomy and is well laid out, even if back-seat passengers can be a bit cramped for legroom. Fairly quiet on the move, but that high position and flexible suspension means rolling on corners, and a bouncy ride on old models may be uncomfortable for some passengers. 1998 Discoveries are now considerably more comfortable and secure on the road.

Practicality ●●●●○

Plenty of room in the load area, which can also take two extra seats. The Discovery is never less than useful.

Driving ●●●●●

Distinction has to be made between old and new models, on- and off-road. Off-road it is brilliant, especially from 1998 with many technical enhancements. On the road, the old model could be quite hard to manoeuvre. 1998 models have lots of gadgets and handle like sports cars.

Performance ●●●○○

Avoid the small 2.0 petrol engine MPI. The V8 is smoother, and smoother still from 1998; not too fast, but ideal for motorway cruising and overtaking. TDI diesel is not quick, but is refined and hard-working.

Economy ●●●○○

Mpg was never a Discovery strong point. Avoid the petrol model. The TDI diesel manages over 30 mpg, though, while the V8 struggles at 17–19 mpg.

Safety ●●●●●

Early models are three-star, with ABS brakes and air bags from 1995. New five-star Discovery has lots more features and technical enhancements as standard.

Security ●●●●●

The older pre-1998 Discovery was only worthy of three stars, it eventually got an alarm and immobiliser by 1995. 1998 models have a five-star system, rated category one by the insurance industry, with high-tech door locks, immobilisers and alarms.

SUM UP

Which model?

1998 vehicles are a huge improvement, but hugely pricey as a used proposition. Older models need to be checked carefully but a five-door TDI is always going to be a popular choice. V8s and three-doors will be cheaper, but long-term, will cost more.

FOR Spacious. Ability.

AGAINST Reliability. Rear overhang.

DOW RATING
●●●●●

Vauxhall Frontera
1991 on

CHECKPOINTS
◆ Water leaks in doors ◆ Damage to underside
◆ Noisy engines ◆ Oil leaks ◆ Noisy wheel bearings

Frontera profile

The three- door Sport and five-door Estate Frontera always has been a low-priced, tough and well-packaged off-roader which is ready for work. However, the all-new model in 1998 saw Vauxhall trying to put right all the handling and reliability problems that affected the old model, while also trying to inject some style into the vehicle. Largely they succeeded.

 Image   ●●●○○

When it comes to rugged charm, the Frontera has that in spades. The body on the new model may be softer, but it still looks the big, butch, off-road part. The Frontera name is well established, but it still lacks the credibility of Land Rover or Jeep, even if it can get close to them off-road.

 Running costs   ●●●○○

Low parts and labour costs make this a cheap off-roader to own. Oil-change service intervals are at a recommended 9/10,000 miles. The 1998 model is even cheaper to service. Resale value is only average. Probably one of the cheapest off-roaders to run simply because it is a mass-market Vauxhall.

Reliability ●●○○○

The old Frontera was a nightmare when it came to reliability. Lots of problems, few related to owner abuse. A new factory and improvements in quality control means that the new Frontera is considerably better.

 Value for money ●●●●○

The Frontera is around in some numbers, so used prices are competitive. Some specifications are a bit basic.

 Comfort ●●●○○

Cramped in the back of the old models, 1998 models have considerably more room. Jiggly ride in the three-door, but the larger estate is much better. Cheap plastics and the low-grade interior are not very inspiring.

 Practicality ●●●○○

A decent-sized boot with good access. On 1998 models the rear window opens, although the rear door is side-hinged to the left, which is a bit clumsy.

 Driving ●●●○○

The old Frontera had vague steering, rolled in corners, but otherwise handled not too badly. 1998 steering is responsive, with less body roll on corners; more refinement on the road and more accomplished off it. Old model is competent: latest gadgets like push-button engagement of four-wheel drive, mean excellent off-road ability.

 Performance ●●●○○

Petrol 2.2 litre offers the best acceleration, with reasonable economy. Small 2.3 turbo diesel is sluggish. The post-1998 V6 offers the best performance, but at the expense of economy.

 Economy ●●●○○

On the whole, Fronteras are not bad, with mid-20s mpg for the petrols and diesels getting around 28 mpg, although reduction in the weight of 1998 Fronteras means 30 mpg.

 Safety ●●●○○

Early Fronteras only offered air bags and ABS brakes as options. Driver and passenger air bags and side impact door beams became standard from 1998. The structure is also claimed to be much stronger than it was before. Four stars, then, for the new version.

 Security ●●●○○

Alarms and immobilisers only from 1995; from 1998, though, a remote keyless entry system is coupled to an excellent deadlock system. Four stars for that.

SUM UP

Which model?

There's a huge difference between the old and new Fronteras. The old model is best seen as a budget workhorse. Although it has its has limitations, an old-model diesel will do a very competent job. The new-model Frontera is a bargain. Despite being flawed, it is a useful car to own.

FOR Running costs. Off-road ability.

AGAINST Reliability. Styling. Unrefined.

DOW RATING
●●●○○

Chrysler Jeep Cherokee

1993 on

CHECKPOINTS

♦ Interiors can be in poor condition ♦ Oil leaks from underside,
especially gearbox and engine ♦ High-mileage smoking engines

Cherokee profile

It was no surprise that Britain took to the friendly American Cherokee, which is good value, well equipped and great to drive. Although it has been substantially revised in 1997, the basic design is dated, which means interior space is limited. However, it is easy to drive and own, important qualities in an off-roader.

Image ●●●●●

For a while the Cherokee was one of the most fashionable off-roaders you could buy. Despite the arrival of Land Rover's Freelander and lots of other competitors, the Jeep still has a lot of credibility. One reason is that it is not too big, and it also has the classic boxy styling which looks so right on the Cherokee.

Running costs ●●●○○

Competitive service and maintenance costs, especially if a buyer is comparing the Cherokee with a Land Rover V8 Discovery. Insurance grouping starts at 12. Resale values have slipped, but demand is still strong for good used examples. The poor petrol economy dramatically effects the longer term costs.

Reliability ●●●●○

Apart from some minor electrical problems, Cherokees have been behaving pretty much faultlessly, and that is unlikely to change. Many problems are only driver-inflicted, especially if used carelessly off-road.

 ## Value for money ●●●○○

Limited numbers on the used market restricts choice. However, Cherokees have always been well packaged. The level of equipment from the 2.5 Sport upwards is comprehensive when it comes to safety, security and electrical fittings. There may even be the balance of their excellent three-year warranty.

 ## Comfort ●●●●○

Fine for those in the nicely shaped front seats, but those in the rear will complain; it is far too cramped for comfort. Build quality is excellent, and a more modern dashboard gives the Cherokee a reassuringly solid feel. The ride is quite good, although it can feel harsh on occasions, but overall it provides a very car-like experience.

 ## Practicality ●●○○○

The big let-down is the lack of interior space. It can feel cramped.

 ## Driving ●●●●●

The easy-to-operate Cherokee has a big advantage in being on the small side. A high driving position is great, but it also feels very nimble and manoeuvrable. The handling is excellent, there is little body roll on corners, it has sharp steering, unusual for an off-roader, and good brakes. Off-road it is just as accomplished. The perfect combination.

 ## Performance ●●●●○

The smallest 2.5 litre petrol is a bit sluggish, although it manages to keep up with most traffic and cruises well enough on the motorway. The 4.0 litre, though, turns the Cherokee into one of the quickest off-roaders, although fuel consumption suffers. The 2.5 diesel is the compromise.

 ## Economy ●●●○○

Mpg is the biggest issue as the 4.0 litre can't better 20 mpg, the 2.5 litre is up to 25 mpg, only the turbo diesel makes a decent stab at 30 mpg.

 ## Safety ●●●●○

Driver air bag from 1994, passenger air bag from 1997. ABS brakes are fitted to the 4.0 litre and limited models. The body was strengthened in 1997.

 ## Security ●●●○○

Vulnerable to attack, there is an engine immobiliser and alarm higher up the range.

SUM UP

Which model?

Turbo diesel is the answer for the economy-minded. Limited specifications are very comprehensive. Petrols are thirsty but the 4.0 is worth having for superb on-road performance.

FOR Equipment. Handling.

AGAINST Cramped. Dated.

DOW RATING
●●●●○

BMW 3-series
1991 on

CHECKPOINTS

♦ Accident damage   ♦ Noisy engines that will be expensive to repair
♦ Altered mileages   ♦ Full service history

3 Series profile

BMW's small executive 3-series effectively set the blueprint which other manufacturers have tried to copy. A combination of quality and driver appeal encompasses a huge range from the hatchback Compact, through to four-door saloons, five-door Touring estates, plus a two-door coupé and convertible. In their own way, each is perfect.

 Image   ●●●●●

BMW stands for superb engineering, sporty handling and great build quality. That is enough to give any model an automatic five-star rating, although some may feel that the entry-level hatchback Compact is a bit downmarket. However, this model range has a blue-chip image and almost everyone aches to own one.

 Running costs   ●●●○○

BMWs are never the cheapest cars to run, although that is usually offset by their reliability and resale value. In recent years, BMW have managed to contain, or reduce, certain parts prices, but main-dealer labour costs are always going to be high. The biggest problem is keeping up with servicing and maintenance costs over the long term.

Reliability ●●●●●

BMW made build-quality mistakes when these 3-series was first launched, but the problems were quickly rectified. Since then they have had an unblemished record, which is likely to continue.

Value for money

Although there are lots of used 3-series on sale, they remain relatively expensive. Buyers also have to avoid low-specification and tired-looking ex-fleet models, which won't have sunroofs and come in bland colours. They may be cheaper to buy, but are difficult to resell.

Comfort

Rear accommodation, especially in the saloons, is tight. Otherwise all the models, especially the six-cylinder ones, are quiet and refined. Excellent front seats, plus a well laid out dashboard and quality feel to the trim make it a very pleasing environment.

Practicality

Decent-sized boot, but Touring estate is not very practical in the conventional estate sense. The Compact is useful, but a squeeze for four.

Driving

One aspect of the 3-series that owners never tire of is the excellent handling. It all comes together in the perfectly laid-out cockpit, where the slick gear change, sweet engines and precise steering deliver inspiring thrills.

Performance

The four-cylinder models will always feel slightly underpowered, whereas the larger sixes are smooth and seductive. The punchy 318I is a good compromise, though, while the 323I and 328I are evenly matched for power. There isn't a bad car in the range, but the high power suits the coupé best.

Economy

Considering BMW's reputation for sportiness, the fuel returns are very good. The petrol 316 and 318I manage 35 mpg, similar to the six-cylinder 323I. Turbo diesel power in 318tds Compact means 47 mpg and 325tds get 41 mpg.

Safety

The 3-series has always been among the safest of small executive cars, and the standard specification includes ABS brakes and, from 1993, driver air bags.

Security

The deadlock system is very difficult to overcome. There is also an electronic engine immobiliser.

SUM UP

Which model?

Only the smallest 316I may disappoint some buyers. The 318 is fine, but smooth six-cylinder models from the 320I onwards are what BMW ownership is all about. Touring estates are a style statement rather than a proper estate.

FOR Refinement. Build quality. Handling.

AGAINST Cramped in the back.

DOW RATING
●●●●●

Jaguar XJ

1986 on

CHECKPOINTS

♦ Damaged panels ♦ Rust ♦ Smoking engine ♦ Service history
♦ Electrical faults ♦ Brakes, suspension and steering wear ♦ Oil leaks
♦ Damaged interior

XJ profile

Well-established range of performance luxury saloons. Square styling in 1986 is not so pretty; the revamp in 1994 is much better. Daimler-badged models are even more sumptuous. They may have some faults, being less than roomy, but when it comes to performance and style, the Jaguar is in a class by itself. As used buys, big depreciation makes them fantastic bargains.

 Image ●●●●●

Even though Jaguar have been through some rocky times, the low, sporting and sleek saloons have always been impressive head-turners, especially since 1994. Now, with their reputation rebuilt, and quality massively improved, the Jaguar character can shine through.

 Running costs ●○○○○

Big service bills are part of the XJ experience, as are big fuel bills. Parts are expensive, although there are lots of specialists and Jaguar salvage yards. Insurance starts at a reasonable group 15 for an old 2.9. If you buy a fairly new XJ, depreciation is horrendous.

Reliability

It is important to distinguish between 1980s Jaguars and those from post-1994. Jaguar reliability has come on in leaps and bounds, thanks to Ford involvement. Now one of the most trustworthy luxury cars you can buy. Older ones can be a nightmare, though.

 ## Value for money

With a Jaguar, you can count on getting an awful lot of luxury car for not very much money. Prices are always low, and even the restyled post-1994 models are very affordable. The only problem is that they keep depreciating. Jaguars also come with a three-year, 60,000-mile warranty, so there may still be some factory guarantee.

 ## Comfort

If a Jaguar is not comfortable, then it is not doing its job. The XJs soak up all the bumps and have a beautiful ride, except for the firmed-up Sport and XJR models. The XJ is in danger of being docked a star for lack of rear legroom; however, the stretched Jaguar- and Daimler-badged versions are the solution.

 ## Practicality

It has a long, but not very deep, boot.

 ## Driving

An update to the dashboard in 1994 made the XJ much more driver-friendly. It is a tight if comfortable fit, although some of the controls look and feel cheap. The handling, though, especially with the tuned Sport versions, is remarkable for such a large car. However hard it gets treated, the XJ remains refined and dignified. Easy to use around town, too.

 ## Performance

Performance is good except for the 2.9 litre.

 ## Economy

Recent improvements have seen 3.2 and 4.0 engines return between 26 and 27 mpg. The XJ12, though, barely manages 18 mpg.

 ## Safety

ABS and driver air bag from 1993, and 1994 revamp added a passenger bag and side bags, among other technical driver aids.

 ## Security

The older cars never had any proper security measures; from 1994, though, there was an engine immobiliser, alarm and eventually a deadlock system.

SUM UP

Which model?

The 3.2 Jaguar is probably the most economical XJ buy. However, it must have a leather trim and a strong colour to be easy to resell. V12s are cheap but may prove impossible to run and resell in the long run. Latest V8 engines have the best long-term prospects. Avoid shabby XJs, however cheap they may be.

FOR Engines. Styling. Performance. Comfort.

AGAINST Cramped in back. Depreciation.

DOW RATING
●●●●○

Audi A4   1995 on

CHECKPOINTS

◆ Service history is essential   ◆ Turbo diesel engines are noisy at high miles   ◆ Hard-used estates with damaged interiors   ◆ Worn engines will produce lots of smoke   ◆ Buy immaculate, never shabby A4s

A4 profile

More proof that Audi could take on BMW and win. In the compact executive class, the A4 is still a desirable alternative to the BMW 3-series. Although the A4 has had minor revisions, it has lost none of its high-quality appeal. For ambitious executives and families after a classy saloon, or stylish Avant estate, the A4 remains the most intelligent choice.

 Image   ●●●●●

The A4 is the model which finally established Audi as one of the most sophisticated, yet understated, manufacturers in the world. The build quality is class-leading, the design superb and the overall packaging faultless. A4s are not brash, but efficient and, when required, exciting cars to own and drive. For many, that is the perfect combination.

 Running costs   ●●●●○

Running costs are always going to be on the higher side, but then it depends what you compare an A4 with. In German executive car terms, the A4 is on the low side, servicing is reasonable, insurance groupings start at just 10, and resale values are among the highest in its class. Long term the A4 may prove increasingly expensive as the design dates and servicing costs escalate.

Reliability ●●●●●

Audi A4s have proved to be extremely reliable, and there is no reason why that situation should change in the future.

Value for money ●●●○○

Expensive to buy from an Audi dealer, but increasing numbers can be found at used car supermarkets. The specification from the entry-level 1.6 is fairly comprehensive. The corrosion warranty at ten years is impressive. What buyers are getting is quality materials and terrific standards of build.

Comfort ●●●●○

The interior provides excellent all-round space, and the seats are well shaped and comfortable. Passengers enjoy the relaxed, supple ride too, although there may be moans from the back seats, where space is a bit more limited.

Practicality ●●●○○

The Avant estate is also a squeeze when it comes to luggage, although the boot layout is logical and quite plush.

Driving ●●●●●

Not much for a driver to complain about with a great range of flexible engines, rapid gear changes and a dashboard which is well laid out and solidly built. The ride is smooth and refined at all times, and getting comfortable for the driver is not a problem. A great place to be.

Performance ●●●●○

The smallest 1.6 is on the slow side, but the engine never sounds as though it is struggling. The 1.8T is more rewarding and the turbo diesels are a useful combination

of economy and performance. The V6 is hugely powerful, but however hard you drive it, it is never less than refined.

Economy ●●●●○

Average fuel consumption only drops below 30 mpg for the complex 2.8 four-wheel drive Quattro. Otherwise 1.6 returns 37 mpg and 1.8 35 mpg. Diesels are very frugal at around 55 mpg.

Safety ●●●●○

The A4 body is immensely strong. Door impact beams, ABS brakes, air bags, strong centre posts and soft interior trim all protect the occupants.

Security ●●●●○

The anti-theft alarm is installed to protect against break-ins. The system includes an engine immobiliser and the central locking is also security-protected. Alloy wheels have security bolts, and the vehicle's identification number is prominently displayed.

SUM UP

Which model?

A very good range of vehicles; the Avant estate is the stylish, rather than practical choice. The 1.6 engine is underpowered, the 1.8 is better, and turbo diesels are nothing short of remarkable.

FOR Build quality. Engines. Comfort. Image.

AGAINST Cramped rear and estate.

DOW RATING
●●●●○

Mercedes 190
1983–93

CHECKPOINTS

♦ Service history is essential ♦ Oil leaks ♦ Altered mileage
♦ Rust indicates a poor repair ♦ Worn brakes, suspension and
steering on a tired example

190 profile

Compact executive cars do not come with a finer pedigree than the 190. All the
qualities of the larger Mercedes saloons in a similar, high-quality package.
There is a wide range of engine and specification options. Small for a Mercedes,
but big-car behaviour. Should last a lifetime.

Image ✦✦✦✦✦

The three-pointed star says it all: quality,
style and respect. It doesn't matter that
the 190 was always at the affordable end of
the Mercedes range, because all people see
is that badge. The fact that the 190 is now
an old car does not matter. Still a very
classy package. Respectable image except
when fitted with nasty bodykits.

Running costs ✦✦✦○○

No Mercedes is cheap to run, and with
6,000-mile service intervals, expenses can
mount up. Lots of independent specialists
can keep costs containable, rather than
parts and labour charges from a Mercedes
dealer. Although older 190s are getting
cheap, a well-maintained example still
depreciates very slowly.

Reliability ●●●●●

Mercedes' well-earned reputation for reliability is embodied in the over-engineered and superbly well-built 190. Money spent on routine maintenance will see these cars sail past the 200,000-mile mark, making them very cheap to run.

  Value for money ●●●○○

Lots of cheap early 190s about, but not all have very high specifications. Ideally a Mercedes should have the 2.0 litre engine, automatic gearbox and a strong metallic colour for resale purposes. 1.8 models with hardly any extras and a manual gearbox don't seem so special.

  Comfort ●●●○○

The driving position is good and the seats may be firm, but they are very supportive. Not very much room in the back, so passengers find it tight. Otherwise the refinement levels are good, with a big-car ride and low noise levels.

  Practicality ●●●○○

The 190 has a good-sized boot, and as an everyday working car is brilliant. Millions of German taxi drivers can't be wrong.

  Driving ●●●●○

A staid rather than sporting Mercedes and that means refinement and comfort are top of the priorities list. Even so, the 190 is capable enough, with good brakes and sharp steering, even though the steering wheel feels as big as a truck's.

  Performance ●●●●○

There are several engine options. The 1.8 and diesels are very sluggish. The 2.0E

model is the best all-rounder. 2.6 six-cylinder is an underrated performance car which is cheap to insure. The flashier 2.5-16 is very un-Mercedes-like and very quick.

  Economy ●●●●○

Good overall economy. Never worse than 30 mpg. Diesels get 40 mpg and the 2.0 petrol a creditable 35 mpg.

  Safety ●●●○○

The 190 may be an old model, but Mercedes have always had a fine reputation for crash safety, and this car has a strong shell. ABS brakes on most models by 1991, and also air bags by 1992.

  Security ●●○○○

Apart from decent door locks, no immobilisers or alarms fitted as standard. Fitting some sort of security device is essential as wherever the Mercedes is used it attracts unwanted attention.

SUM UP

Which model?

2.0E with an automatic transmission, a nice colour and sunroof is a safe, easy-to-resell purchase. Diesels are fine if you are not in a hurry and intend to keep the 190 for ever. The 2.6 is an underrated small performance saloon. Lots to choose from, but avoid shabby examples.

FOR Reliability. Quality. Image.

AGAINST Tired examples. Cramped rear. Slow 1.8 and diesels.

DOW RATING
●●●●○

Mazda MX5 1990 on

C H E C K P O I N T S

♦ Vandal damage to hood or body.

♦ Cheap Japanese import Eunos, badged as MX5s   ♦ No service history

MX5 profile

The roadster that started the 90s drop-top revival. Cheeky retro 60s styling, this is the most capable, yet easy to own, open-top car you can buy. Performance is good, as is the ride, making it the most sensible choice if you plan on going topless. So popular that the British market has become flooded with high-specification Japanese Eunos models.

 Image ✸✸✸✸✸

Mazda took the 60s sports-car ingredients of simplicity, style and value, then combined all that with modern car reliability. Restyled in 1988, the MX5 has lost some of its original charm, along with pop-up headlamps, but it remains a modern classic.

 Running costs ✸✸✸○○

Mazda saloon-car servicing costs. The insurance grouping starts at a reasonable 11. MX5 had a fabulous resale value, although this has been affected by the imported Japanese Eunos. Restyled 1998 model not affected yet. One of the cheapest sports cars you can run.

Reliability ✱✱✱✱✱

Unlike the 60s sports cars it was influenced by, the MX5 has been faultlessly reliable. Only owner abuse has caused any problems. Provided an MX5 is not used as a fair-weather car and locked away untouched every season, it runs like clockwork.

  Value for money ✱✱✱○○

The MX5 is getting more affordable as more Eunos (MX5 in Japan) are imported, which depresses prices. Don't get confused between the two. The British cars have a fairly basic specification.

  Comfort ✱✱✱✱○

The great thing about the MX5 is that it is not a compromise convertible, so driver and passenger do not have to suffer for going topless. The ride and refinement levels are good, plus the easy-erect hood all mean that owning an MX5 is a doddle. Good sports seats, nicely retro dashboard and a nice ride at normal road speeds.

  Practicality ✱✱✱○○

Good-quality trim, comfortable seats and a larger boot on the 1998 model make the car a very practical proposition. Excellent and simple hood transforms the MX5 into a snug coupé.

  Driving ✱✱✱✱✱

Surely one of the best sports cars of all time, with excellent and precise handling. Heavily revised 1998 MX5 is now even more fun to drive. It grips enthusiastically on corners and there is little flexing of the bodywork, which spoils many sports cars' handling characteristics. Power-assisted steering is perfectly balanced, and allows the car to be precisely positioned on the road.

  Performance ✱✱✱✱○

The MX5 is not about speed; with the 1.6 and 1.8 engines, there is just enough power to have fun. They feel quicker than they are. Both units are ably assisted by the slick gear change, which means smooth, yet fast progress.

  Economy ✱✱✱✱○

Average fuel consumption hovers around the mid-30s mpg.

  Safety ✱✱✱○○

Apart from side impact protection beams in 1995 there are no other safety fittings, but the MX5 is still one of the safest small sports cars you can buy. On 1998 MX5s, air bags are standard, ABS brakes are optional.

  Security ✱✱○○○

Engine immobiliser on some special editions.

SUM UP

Which model?

Original 1.6 now feels slow, but will be cheap. 1.8 probably the best engine option. Standard steel wheels look awful, and specifications can be basic. Quite a few special-edition models around, but don't pay too much for them.

FOR Great steering. Handling. Styling. Falling prices.

AGAINST Eunos imports badged as MX5s.

DOW RATING
✱✱✱✱✱

Porsche 911 1963 on

CHECKPOINTS

♦ Accident damage   ♦ Smoky engines   ♦ Service history a must

911 profile

Legend. Icon. Supercar. Plaudits are something that this Porsche has had no trouble picking up over the years. It is also a used-car legend, with constant demand, a reputation for being built like a bank vault and always holding its value. Constantly improved over the years, early examples are for enthusiasts only. For many it is a sports-car dream come true.

 Image   ✦✦✦✦✦

Owners of Porsches in general and the 911 in particular provoke one of two responses: brilliant or flash. Either way, it proves that the owner has money, but also taste. Most of all, the 911 has a proper racing pedigree: after all, they still win races. Anyone with only a passing interest in cars knows what a 911 looks like and also wants one, badly.

 Running costs   ✦✦✦○○

911s must be looked after, but then they will look after you by never breaking down. Huge network of specialists can side-step Porsche main-agent parts prices and labour rates. Even so, maintenance is high. Insurance is too, mostly group 20, although a low-mileage classic-car policy may be the answer. Probably the cheapest high-performance car to run.

Reliability

The 911 really is a usable supercar which will do the weekday commute and even some weekend track-day fun without a murmur, provided service history is up to date and the owner never skimps on a thing. It is essential to buy a good example in the first place.

 Value for money

The only thing that counts against all 911s is the asking price. Few bargains at dealers, but some private deals make sense. It pays to be patient. There are increasing numbers of left-hand drive imports in the country to satisfy demand, priced well below right-hand drive versions. Provided it's in good condition and you don't mind sitting on the left, a very cost-effective 911.

 Comfort

Not a Porsche strong point. Ventilation is marginal, dashboard and control layout is eccentric, to say the least. Not only that, it is noisy too. The ride is also very harsh. Yet again, that is all part of the appeal.

 Practicality

Boot is in the front and not huge. Rear seats are marginal and best left to hand luggage or very small children. Practical for a supercar, though.

 Driving

Never less than exciting. Older ones are pretty evil and not for the novice driver; they must be treated with respect, the Turbo being the worst in this respect. Later Carrera 2s and 4s are easier to tame. Essentially the rear-mounted engine is in the wrong place, but for the enthusiast that's the fun of it.

 Performance

Shattering. Even an automatic, or Tiptronic as Porsche call it, gets to 60 mph in just over six seconds and only runs out of puff just short of 160 mph. Turbo gets way beyond 170 mph.

 Economy

Across the range it averages from the mid- to low-20s mpg.

 Safety

In the wrong hands a 911 is dangerous. Otherwise the body is strong and it has air bags from 1993 plus ABS brakes.

 Security

Locks are OK, but alarms and immobilisers not fitted as standard until 1994.

SUM UP

Which model?

For someone who knows what they are buying, any 911 is a five-star buy. 80s Carreras are reasonable value, anything much older is for enthusiasts. The Turbo is overrated. Later models are much more novice-friendly. Always get expert help when choosing and buying.

FOR Build. Performance. Character. Image.

AGAINST Handling. Road noise. Expensive.

DOW RATING

MGF

1995 on

CHECKPOINTS

- ◆ Check hood fit and condition ◆ Look for water leaks
- ◆ Upholstery damage ◆ Accident damage

MGF profile

Few MGs in recent years have actually deserved to wear the famous octagonal badge, but the F does. Rather than taking a conventional route, Rover have been brave and put the engine behind the driver. This and other technical innovations have helped create one of the most refined and easy-to-live-with roadsters ever built.

 Image ●●●●●

An MG can only be one thing: a sports car. The MGF may be a bit softer than some competitors, but despite the long lay-off, the MG badge still counts for something. Rover have cleverly combined tradition and technology. This is no poser's convertible; the MGF has real style and substance.

 Running costs ●●●●○

Good news – the MGF should not cost a fortune to run. Servicing costs are no more than a small Rover hatchback. It is group 12 insurance for the 1.8 and 14 for the VVC. Depreciation is very slow, although now an MGF is proving to be less of an investment with lots being re-imported from Japan.

Reliability ●●●○○

Early reports have highlighted some recurrent troubles. Most have been engineered out, but leaking hoods and electrical problems feature among them.

 ### Value for money ●●●●○

After being difficult to find and expensive, there are more MGFs around than ever and prices are falling. They have a good level of equipment and are very good value when compared with a Lotus Elise, or BMW Z3.

 ### Comfort ●●●●○

Convertibles, especially small ones, do not have to be comfortable to win admirers, but the MGF manages to be refined at all times, whether the hood is up or down. The trim is a bit plasticky, the finish not bad, but because there is no driver's-seat height adjustment, tall drivers may find it cramped.

 ### Practicality ●●●○○

There is a fair-sized boot situated behind the engine compartment. Hardly a load-lugger, but easy to live with.

 ### Driving ●●●●●

There is plenty of grip, it always feels safe and can be easily pushed to the limit. At other times the excellent suspension system and very taut body provides a luxury-saloon-car ride. It is the perfect combination.

 ### Performance ●●●●○

The 1.8 version has enough acceleration for the less demanding driver, getting to 60 mph in fewer than ten seconds and having a top speed of almost 120 mph. Most new and used buyers, though, opt for the wonderful VVC, which can reach 130 mph. This is only hampered by a less-than-slick gear change. Even so, the VVC can get up to 60 mph in just over seven seconds.

 ### Economy ●●●○○

Fuel economy averages an impressive 37 mpg for both engine options.

 ### Safety ●●●○○

Driver air bag is standard and passenger air bag is optional. ABS brakes are only standard on the VVC. Despite the engine being mid-mounted, there is no reduction in crash protection and it complies with all prevailing safety regulations.

 ### Security ●●●●○

Deadlocks offer excellent security with the hood erected. However, convertibles are always going to be vulnerable. Additional protection is offered by an alarm and engine immobiliser.

SUM UP

Which model?

The 1.8 is underrated and cheaper. It may not be fast, but it still looks the sports car part and will be ideal for most buyers. The high-performance VVC has a higher resale value and will be more in demand, though.

FOR Refined. Comfortable. Practical.

AGAINST Minor build-quality niggles.

DOW RATING
●●●●○

MGB

1962–80

CHECKPOINTS

♦ Serious rust on sills, floors, suspension ♦ Sub-standard restoration
♦ Worn, smoky engine, noisy gearbox and broken suspension are easier to replace than rotted body

MGB profile

One of the most enduring and loved British sports cars of all time. Available first as an open-topped roadster, then as a coupé, the MGB GT, and also as a high-performance V8 coupé. All models were elegant, practical and versatile when new and all those qualities still apply today. One of the soundest, though not necessarily cheapest, classic buys which couldn't be easier to look after, or live with.

Image ●●●●●

Quintessential British sports car styling has hardly dated. Never mind the string-backed gloves and tweed cap MG image of old, the MGB can still outpose the new generation of 90s convertibles without really trying. Makes a fantastic noise as well, not something that modern regulations allow.

Running costs ●●●●●

Brilliant news about MGBs is that every last part, from body shells to engines, gearboxes and little rubber grommets can be bought brand new off the shelf. Simple mechanicals mean that DIY servicing, even for the novice, is possible. Classic-car, limited-mileage insurance is low. Depreciation is also minimal.

Reliability

Provided the MGB you buy is a sound one, it should not give too many problems. It obviously needs more maintenance than a modern car, but simple 60s mechanicals mean problems are usually minor. Rust, if it gets a hold, is a major worry.

 ### Value for money

Despite there being lots around, MGBs, particularly roadsters, are never cheap. In fact, the GTs are better value. Also, everyone wants the classic chrome bumper look rather than the 'rubber bumper' models from 1974, which were built to comply with US regulations. Not so pretty, but cheaper and more practical with fewer parking dents.

 ### Comfort

Roadsters are reasonably civilised, even with the hood up. Quite noisy, but roomy enough for two. The hard-top GTs are even better. They ride well and are much more solid and refined, especially the V8.

 ### Practicality

A very good-sized boot on the roadster, plus extra space behind the seats. The GT is basically a hatchback, with a decent amount of usable luggage room. This is a classic that you really can use every day.

 ### Driving

Easy enough to drive. The steering may feel heavy if you are used to modern cars, and the gear change is not that slick, but the MGB is safe and secure provided it isn't pushed too hard. It is easy to find this model's limits and then stick within them. Later rubber-bumper cars are not so proficient in the handling department and need upgrading.

 ### Performance

Not that quick really, although the exhaust note sounds very meaningful. Just over 100 mph, only reasonably brisk acceleration, modern hatchbacks will leave an MGB standing. Heavier GTs are even slower. V8s are quite swift, delivering 125 mph.

 ### Economy

Most MGBs average around 25–30 mpg.

 ### Safety

A strong body, but this is still a 60s design. A lot of protection offered by the long bonnet and the 'rubber bumper' models can withstand low-speed (5 mph) impacts without damage.

 ### Security

Open-top roadsters are very vulnerable. It is essential for owners to at least fit a good engine immobiliser.

SUM UP

Which model?

Avoid automatics. Avoid earliest versions, which are for enthusiasts only. From 1965 the MGB had a better engine. Rubber bumpers don't look as good, but will be cheaper. GTs are practical, all-year-round MGBs.

FOR Cheap parts. Easy maintenance. Lots of choice. Character.

AGAINST Slow. Expensive. Common. Rust.

DOW RATING

Volkswagen Beetle

1949 on

CHECKPOINTS

- ◆ Rust on the wings, around the suspension, engine and doors
- ◆ Engines very durable ◆ Look out for bodged restoration and the convertible, which is not a genuine 'factory' model

Beetle profile

A model that needs no introduction and which has been around for over fifty years. Available as a two-door saloon and a convertible, more than twenty-two million have been sold worldwide. Not for everyone; it is cramped, noisy, but utterly reliable. What's more, you can still buy brand-new ones fresh from the factory in Mexico!

 Image ◆◆◆◆◆

Love or loathe them, nobody can ignore the Beetle. It is now part of popular culture and quite rightly so. The familiar shape still manages to raise a smile after all these years. Is it any surprise that VW have decided to update it with a brand-new model?

 Running costs ◆◆◆◆○

Once a Beetle is running properly, costs ought to be containable. Spares are fairly cheap and there is a worldwide network of specialists. Classic-car insurance is low. However, buy a Beetle which needs a lot of care and restoration costs can escalate.

Reliability ●●●●○

There isn't a great deal to go wrong on a Beetle. The engine is very tough, although regular maintenance is essential, and any bodges soon turn into major problems. Build quality was always excellent, although once rust gets a hold the Beetle will need major refurbishment to pass its MOT.

 Value for money ●●●○○

There are plenty to choose from, and the big problem is picking the right one. Older ones are not cheap, but the better later 1302 and 1303 series are less collectible, so fine value. Genuine convertibles always cost a fortune.

 Comfort ●●○○○

You'll get used to it. The thrashy engine, cramped interior and slow, noisy progress are all part of the charm of the Beetle. You either learn to love the spartan interior and all the noises that go with it, or you buy something else. It's a squeeze for four.

 Practicality ●●○○○

Not a great deal of luggage room under the bonnet, except with the more prominent nose of the later models.

 Driving ●●○○○

Rudimentary suspension and rear engine layout can mean tricky handling in the wet; you will skid! Otherwise slow, sure and perfectly designed to sit on the motorway at 70 mph, if you can stand the noise.

 Performance ●●○○○

What performance? Acceleration is marginal, the Beetle just gathers speed slowly but sure. Later versions will manage 80 mph maximum, but essentially they are cruising machines which will drone on mile after mile at 60–70 mph.

 Economy ●●●○○

Not as outstanding as you might imagine. As the Beetle got more refined and the engine larger, the fuel consumption dropped from 37 mpg down to 27 mpg by 1970.

 Safety ●●○○○

The handling might get you into trouble, even if its performance wouldn't. Good build quality means reasonable crash protection, although remember the design dates back to the 30s.

 Security ●○○○○

Door locks are easy to overcome. Security measures are negligible on the Beetle so it is up to you. Make sure you at least fit some sort of visual deterrent such as a steering lock.

SUM UP

Which model?

Avoid early models before 1967. They are for enthusiasts and only had troublesome, low-voltage electrics. Late models like the 1302 and 1303 are the most practical and often the cheapest. The convertible is stylish, but very expensive.

FOR Running costs. Style. Charm.

AGAINST Cramped. Expensive to buy. Slow.

DOW RATING
●●●●○○

Morris Minor

1948–71

CHECKPOINTS

- ◆ Rust in the floor, around the suspension, in wings, on sills
- ◆ Rotten wood on the half-timbered estate ◆ Is the convertible genuine, or a converted saloon?

Minor profile

A British institution, the Morris Minor has provided no-nonsense transportation as a three- and four-door saloon, a half-timbered estate (the Traveller) a convertible and also a van and pick-up. Versatile, practical, affordable and surprisingly still very usable thirty years after they went out of production. Genuine, low-cost motoring.

 Image ✦✦✦✦✦

District nurse. Rural vet. Local vicar. Miss Marple. It doesn't matter who is behind the wheel, because the Minor has never been more fashionable. It may look eccentric, but it is one of the most sensible cars you can run.

 Running costs ✦✦✦✦✦

Like so many classic cars, there is a whole cottage industry of specialists who keep costs low. Combine that with classic insurance, virtually nil depreciation and good economy, and this is one of the cheapest cars to run, ever.

Reliability ●●●●●

The simplicity of the Minor means that an example maintained in good condition should not let the owner down. Enthusiasts get to know the weak spots, but overall, faultless. The fact that it is easy to work on adds to its appeal.

  Value for money ●●●●○

Still not overpriced, especially the four-door saloon. It is a different matter with some of the smarter Travellers and highly prized convertibles. Even so, large original production and large number of survivors ensure that Minors never cost too much. Beware the bodged restoration, or disguised rot box.

  Comfort ●●●○○

Not much comfort by modern standards. The seats are not supportive and the engine noise is going to be intrusive. Luckily, there is plenty that can be done if the Minor is to be used every day. Fitting more modern seats, quietening the engine and other modernisations can improve matters.

  Practicality ●●●●○

It carries four people without a problem. The cheaper four-door offers more flexibility. As an everyday car, the Minor is far from temperamental. Reasonable boot and very practical load space in the Traveller.

  Driving ●●●●○

Even though the early versions are under-powered, it is immediately apparent that the Minor is a sporty car to drive with very positive steering and nicely firm suspension. Around town, the steering may seem heavy by modern standards, but if Miss Marple could handle it, so can you.

  Performance ●●●○○

The Minor is not a fast car; this is particularly so with early small-engined versions. Even by the time the Minor had an 1100cc engine, 70 mph would be too noisy and 60 mph just about bearable, making 50 mph its ideal speed. There are plenty of engine modifications which will transform the performance.

  Economy ●●●●○

Fuel returns are reasonable, between 30 and 35 mpg.

  Safety ●●○○○

The Minor won't get the driver into trouble, but its age counts against it in a crash.

  Security ●○○○○

None. Installing some theft prevention is essential.

SUM UP

Which model?

Avoid earliest collectors' Minors and stick to Minor 1000 from 1962 on with its larger engine. Convertibles have to be originals, or professional conversions, while four-doors are undervalued, so cheap. Travellers can be expensive and must be in top condition, as half-timbered rear end is structural.

FOR Practical. Easily modified.

AGAINST Rust. Bodged examples.

DOW RATING
●●●●●

DEALS on WHEELS
Alternatively ...

We couldn't get every car we considered a good buy into our *Deals on Wheels* Top Fifty (see pages 31–131). So, if you didn't see the car of your dreams on the previous pages, or couldn't afford the cars you did see there, here are a few runners-up that are worth considering. For every car there are always plenty of perfectly capable alternatives. From the pocket-money priced Fiat Panda to the sexy Ford Puma, once again there is something for everyone.

City Cars

Daihatsu Curore   1997–9

Cheap when new, very cheap when used, plus it may still have the balance of its three-year warranty. These three- and five-door models are small and very easy to park. The tiny engine is noisy at speed, but perfect around town. Reliable and safe, with a standard driver air bag and, despite cheap interior trim, very cheerful indeed.

Fiat Panda   1981–95

Motoring at its most basic with this three-door hatch. Not very comfortable, but economy and running costs could not be lower. No safety features and no security. Buy the most recent model you can afford. Stick to 90s examples – at least as many 80s Pandas will have rotted away.

SEAT Marbella   1990–95

Spanish-built version of the Panda. Does not have the 'image' of Fiat, so very cheap. Like the Panda, very cheaply built, but has the same ultra-low running cost advantages.

SEAT Arosa   ★★★★★   1997

Spanish version of the VW Lupo. Not so stylish, but just as well built. Feels like a proper grown-up car with good safety features, although an air bag will be an option. Quite cheap because of low image.

Suzuki Wagon R+   ★★★○○   1997 on

An oddball offering which is basically a five-door micro people mover. Three-year warranty from new, suprisingly practical and seats four in relative comfort. Lots of headroom, although not everyone likes the high-rise styling. Operates well in built-up areas, but not many on sale.

Small Hatchbacks

Citroen AX 1987–96

Three- and five-door cars related to the Peugeot 205 and 106, but without the style, or higher prices. Lightweight, but very economical and comfortable to drive. Feels flimsy. Stick to 90s examples, especially the revised models from September 1991.

Fiat Uno 1983–95

Very practical and, if looked after, reliable hatchback. Very roomy, although it can be noisy. Cheap insurance and parts costs, provided the high-performance turbo is avoided. Stick to 90s models. 1.0ie Fire is slow but reliable and easy to maintain.

Mazda 121 1996 on

British-built version of the Ford Fiesta. Has a three-year new-car warranty. Like the Fiesta, a state-of-the-art small hatch, but used examples need a careful comparison with any similar Ford-badged models on sale when it comes to price and specification. Could be a bargain, but longer-term, harder to resell.

Kia Pride 1991 on

This Korean version of an old Mazda is very cheap, practical and reliable, although not the last word in style, or refinement. Big fuel economy a bonus, but must be cheap to be really worthwhile. Buy the 1.3 version.

Nissan Micra 1983–93

The old model Micra is not that safe, or secure, but is so reliable and cheap to run. Provided the model is not a tired ex-driving school example and has been looked after, the Micra makes the ideal bargain buy. Not a patch on the new-model Micra, for quality, but otherwise a good old-fashioned bargain banger.

Renault 5 1989–98

Dates back to the early 70s, and arguably the first 'supermini' small hatch. Very economical, although older versions rust to bits and have all sorts of electrical problems. Buy 90s models badged as Campus. Noisy, cramped, but a comfortable ride and perfect for those on a tight budget.

SEAT Ibiza 1993 on

Spanish-built version of the VW Polo and almost as good. Low-image badge keeps prices low. Equipment levels are good and safety levels up to modern standards. Heavy, so all are slow apart from the GTI versions. Very underrated and often underpriced.

Toyota Starlet 1990 on

Dull range of hatchbacks, despite the name. Build quality and reliability is outstanding, though, and revamped model, from 1996 are much safer and more stylish. Basically a no-worries purchase which will do a decent job.

Volkwagen Polo 1981–94

The old-model Polo is still worth considering. Not the most comfortable small car, with a rough ride, and heavy steering makes parking a pain. Revised 1990 range is a big improvement, though. Very practical and solid and great value for money if cheap.

Small Cars

Daewoo Nexia 1995–7

Underneath is an old Vauxhall Astra, but never mind. These cars are well packaged with low insurance and running costs. They are cheap to buy too, and the mechanicals are obviously well proven. Well cared for models sold privately will last a lifetime.

Fiat Tipo 1988–95

Very underrated and now very cheap. The galvanised body should mean no rust. Good fuel economy and fabulous interior space make it a very practical buy. Minor electrical upsets, but on the whole very reliable. It is also fun to drive and from 1993 and 1994 has modern safety features, including air bag and side impact beams.

Honda Civic 1991–5

Huge and quite baffling range of saloons, hatchbacks and coupés. Never that cheap, they are high-quality and ultra-reliable cars which, when looked after, never go wrong. Dull image, although there are some exciting performance versions in the range, such as, the Vti.

Mazda 323 1991–8

Distinctively styled, with pop-up headlamps, these saloons are the quality alternative to a dull Escort. Can be expensive, though, and running costs, as well as insurance, are on the high side. Very reliable, and from 1994 much improved for safety and performance.

Nissan Almera 1995 on

Often overlooked, but a sound, small family car which is practical and well equipped. The performance is good, as are the comfort levels. Styling is dull, but that keeps prices low. Safe and very sensible indeed.

Renault 19   **1989–96**

Very affordable and hard-working range of saloons and hatchbacks. Cheaper than an Escort or Astra, but just as capable and with a touch more flair. Uprated models from 1992 are better built. Very roomy, comfortable and with the 1.4 version, remarkable fuel economy.

Toyota Corolla   **1992–7**

One of the longest-running ranges on sale; that's because its reputation for reliability and durability is well deserved. Very dull to look at and nothing special to drive, but lots of room inside and utterly reliable. A typical Japanese stress-free purchase.

Family Cars

Chrysler Neon
  1996 on

Bargain American car when new, ought to be equally cheap used. Very well packaged, with everything buyers want as standard, including automatic gearbox and a three-year warranty. Not a lot around, though. A bit cramped in the back, not refined, but great if cheap.

Hyundai Lantra
  1991 on

A Korean range of saloons which are Mitsubishi-based and therefore very reliable. They are well built and well equipped, too. Good levels of safety for such a cheap car, and a major 1995 revamp turned it into an even more impressive budget car.

Mazda 626
  1992–7

Anonymous car, with brilliant practical qualities. Very well built, reliable and with fine performance. An executive quality car, but going for some very ordinary prices now. Lots of room inside, very safe and also a good level of security. Should not be overlooked.

Peugeot 405
  1988–96

Spacious and stylish, the 405 was a popular fleet car in the 80s and 90s; a real alternative to a dull old Sierra. Reliability marks it down because of niggly faults. Otherwise for comfort, practicality (especially the estate) and sheer driving pleasure, few cars offer better value.

Peugeot 406
  1996 on

Superb family saloon car, or estate, with generous levels of standard equipment, which combine with excellent interior space and good handling to make this a great all-rounder. Proving reliable, and because it is a fleet car, there are lots around and prices are low.

Renault Laguna 1994 on

This is a spacious, stylish and comfortable hatchback and estate car. Has proved to be a popular fleet car, which means there are lots around at low prices. Average reliability, but in practical terms, spacious and easy to live with, being good fun to drive.

Volkswagen Passat 1988–7

Useful, yet underrated saloon which offers huge amount of space and reliability. Respected estates are more expensive and just as rugged. Boring to look at, fine to drive, but what really impresses is the sheer quality of construction and feeling that it will last for ever.

People Movers

Chrysler Voyager 1997 on

European-built, but American-designed where it was the first people mover. Very roomy, especially larger Grand model. Lots of equipment, but fuel costs are on the high side. A safe, sensible and cost-effective buy.

Toyota Previa 1990 on

Very large, very futuristic and one of the best of the older people-mover breed. Comfortable, reliable and, unlike some rivals, it can take passengers' luggage too. Getting cheaper and shouldn't be overlooked.

Off-roaders

Daihatsu Fourtrak 1985 on

If all you really want is a hard-working, cheap-to-run and tough three-door estate, here it is. Fine reputation among the rural community. Not very civilised as a car, but very practical as an off-roader.

Isuzu Trooper 1988–98

One of the most honest off-roaders you can buy. Not a luxury vehicle for posing, but a proper mud-plugger which is tough and so much cheaper than its rivals.

Mitsubishi Shogun 1991

This is a Range Rover rival which costs so much less. Also much more reliable. Lots of standard equipment and very comfortable on the road. Parts and servicing are costly, though.

Toyota RAV-4 1994

Not a proper off-roader in the accepted sense. Fashionable, but still functional. Easy to drive, a pleasure on the tarmac, although limited ability off-road. For most buyers that is the perfect combination. Great performance, getting cheaper to buy and very reliable.

Executive Cars

Audi A6 1994 on

An 'affordable' alternative to the medium-sized Mercedes and BMWs, which is safe, solid and stylish. Early examples up to 1997 were a makeover of an earlier model, but it was still outstanding in terms of comfort and refinement. Lots of safety and security features. Recommended.

BMW 5-series 1988–96

Set the standard for this class of car. Superbly well made, refined and reliable. Can become hard to find good examples at the right price; bigger engines in 535 and 540 make them cheaper. Smaller-engined 518 is inappropriate. The Touring estate is not that big. Impressive, but pricey to run.

Mercedes E Class 1985–95

A hugely respected range of saloons and estates which are comfortable, reliable and durable. A large enough car for five, it will last a lifetime if properly maintained. Very safe too.

Saab 9000 1985–99

Underrated executive hatchbacks and saloons with plenty of standard equipment and, in turbo form, no shortage of performance. Hatchback is as roomy as most estate cars. Very safe, but parts and servicing are costly and reliability becomes suspect with age.

Vauxhall Omega 1994 on

This German-built saloon and estate is very affordable. A fleet car, with a lot of executive class, good styling, lots of equipment and plenty of room. Smooth engines and, best of all, low prices. Shame the Vauxhall image is so low.

Volvo 850/S and V70 1994 on

An exciting and never stodgy car, these saloons and estates are spacious and durable. More affordable than the BMW/Mercedes competition, and not far behind in image terms. Great to drive and easy to own.

Sports Cars

Ford Puma 1997 on

Has been an expensive used buy, but it is now becoming affordable. Underneath that distinctive body is a humble Fiesta, but you would never know it. Great to look at, fantastic to drive and, because it is a Ford, easy to own.

Toyota MR2 1990 on

Lots of unofficial imports flooding in from Japan have pushed prices for this remarkable little car down. Know what you are buying, though, and you get a baby Ferrari which is reliable and cost-effective to run.

Volkswagen Corrado 1989–96

Underneath it is an old Golf, but demand for this coupé remains high and it is easy to see why. Brilliant performance, easy to drive and economical to own. High prices mean resale is not a problem, but there are lots of tatty examples around.

Classic Cars

Jaguar Mark 2 1959–67

'Cops and robbers' image, but the looks are seductive, the performance outstanding and interior sumptuous. Shame about the rampant rust. Expensive to restore, but the collapse in classic car prices has made pristine examples affordable again.

Alfa Romeo Spider 1967–93

Ultimate 60s Italian sports car, as featured in *The Graduate*. Updated over the years, although rampant rust is always around. Can be very unreliable. Some recent Californian imports are cheap, but need to be checked carefully.

Rover 3500 1968–76

Forget all the latest retro-styled Rovers; this was a forward-looking, thoroughly modern and, for the time, very safe car. Powerful, compact and probably a little cramped inside, it can still keep up with today's traffic. Becoming more collectable, but still relatively cheap.

DEALS on WHEELS Buyer's Checklists

Always look at the car in clear, dry conditions and wear old clothes. Take a copy of this book and a pen and paper. Most important of all, take a friend. They can stop you making a mistake and will be a useful extra pair of eyes and ears. Never look at a car in the rain, in the dark, or where access to it is restricted. Never allow yourself to be rushed.

BEFORE YOU BUY

- What's your buying budget? £_____

- Will you be borrowing? Yes ☐ No ☐

  If yes, from whom? _____

  At what APR rate? _____

- What sort of car do you want? _____

  _____

  _____

  _____

- After consulting the DOW Top 50, what's your shortlist?

  1 _____

  2 _____

  3 _____

- What are your best insurance quotes?

  £ _____ Company _____

  £ _____ Company _____

  £ _____ Company _____

- Have you sold your car yet? Yes ☐ No ☐

- How much did you get for it? £_____

- Or are you part exchanging? Yes ☐ No ☐

*Congratulations. Now you can actually
start looking for your next car ...*

CAR BUYER'S COMPANION

Car/Owner Details

- Make/model _____
- Registration number _____
- Colour _____
- Interior _____
- Year _____
- Specification. Leather, electric windows, alloy wheels, etc. ...
  _____
  _____
  _____

- Owner's name and address and telephone number_____
  _____
  _____
  _____

- Mileage when owner purchased _____
- Why is car being sold? _____
  _____

Paperwork

- **Service history?**   Yes ☐ No ☐
- Complete?   Yes ☐ No ☐
- Relates to the same vehicle?   Yes ☐ No ☐
- Garage contact numbers?   Yes ☐ No ☐
- Last serviced _____

DOW Buyer's Checklists

- **MOT certificate?**   Yes ☐ No ☐
- How many?   _____
- Watermarks?   Yes ☐ No ☐
- Alterations?   Yes ☐ No ☐
- Mileage on certificates _____

- **V5 registration?**   Yes ☐ No ☐
- Watermarks?   Yes ☐ No ☐
- Mistakes or alterations?   Yes ☐ No ☐
- Private sale? Proof of the seller's identity and address. Yes ☐ No ☐
- Does it match V5?   Yes ☐ No ☐
- Previous owner's address _____
  _____
  _____

- Check V5 against vehicle number plate   Yes ☐ No ☐
- Vehicle identification numbers (VIN) – under bonnet
  on plate, stamped on body, maybe on windows   Yes ☐ No ☐
- Engine number, stamped on a prominent part of the engine Yes ☐ No ☐
- Have the numbers been tampered with?   Yes ☐ No ☐
- Insurance documents?   Yes ☐ No ☐

- Hole in the carpet on the driver's side?   Yes ☐ No ☐
- Are screws holding the dashboard in place worn or scratched?   Yes ☐ No ☐
- Does the steering wheel look out of alignment?   Yes ☐ No ☐
- Are the numbers even on the mileage reading?   Yes ☐ No ☐
- Is there an exclusion clause stuck over the speedometer?   Yes ☐ No ☐

Under the bonnet (cold engine)

- Examine dipstick. Correct level?   Yes ☐ No ☐
- Colour – black, dirty, or burnt?   Yes ☐ No ☐
- Oil filler cap. Clean? Black treacle? White sludge?   Yes ☐ No ☐
- Open the radiator cap. Brown water? White deposits?   Yes ☐ No ☐
- Look underneath: oil or water leaks?   Yes ☐ No ☐
- Get friend to start the engine. Noises? Describe them. _____

  _____

  _____

- Exhaust. Ask friend to rev hard then back off suddenly.
  Lots of blue smoke?   Yes ☐ No ☐

Drive the Car

Car must have a current MOT, and you must be insured to drive it. Turn radio off so you can hear what is happening. Go for a proper drive for at least an hour. Try to experience as many road conditions as possible, from town to motorway.

- Switch on the ignition. Warning lights extinguished?   Yes ☐ No ☐
- Does it take long to start?   Yes ☐ No ☐
- Any rough running or strange noises?   Yes ☐ No ☐
- Power steering. Turn wheel from lock to lock.
  Squeals, strange judders?   Yes ☐ No ☐

Manual gearbox

- First gear. Difficult to engage?　　　　　　　Yes ☐ No ☐

- Noise?　　　　　　　Yes ☐ No ☐

- Free play in the lever?　　　　　　　Yes ☐ No ☐

- With the gears in neutral, press clutch pedal.
  Whirring noises?　　　　　　　Yes ☐ No ☐

- Clutch, put the handbrake on and engage first: does it stall?　Yes ☐ No ☐

Automatic gearbox

- Smooth, fast, silent changes?　　　　　　　Yes ☐ No ☐

- Accelerate, does the gearbox change down smoothly?　Yes ☐ No ☐

Brakes

- Apply as you pull away. Dragging sounds?　　Yes ☐ No ☐

- Intermittent rubbing?　　　　　　　Yes ☐ No ☐

- ABS warning light on/off soon after engine started?　Yes ☐ No ☐

Steering

- Juddering?　　　　　　　Yes ☐ No ☐

- Does it pull to one side?　　　　　　　Yes ☐ No ☐

- On corners, or when turned from lock to lock,
  is there a clicking sound?　　　　　　　Yes ☐ No ☐

Suspension

- Clonks, bangs and bouncing over rough ground?　Yes ☐ No ☐

- Ride in the back of the car. Noises?　　　Yes ☐ No ☐

Dashboard

- Flickering warning lights?   Yes ☐ No ☐

- Temperature gauge behaviour. Hot, cold, not moved?   _____

Accelerate

- Is there blue smoke in the rear mirror?   Yes ☐ No ☐

- Any squeals?   Yes ☐ No ☐

- Whistling turbo (if fitted)?   Yes ☐ No ☐

After the drive

- Leaks in engine bay and underneath?   Yes ☐ No ☐

- Noises from the engine?   Yes ☐ No ☐

Sum Up – Rate this car out of 10

Documentation	/10
Exterior	/10
Interior	/10
Mechanical	/10
Road test	/10

Is this car worth a professional second opinion? Yes ☐ No ☐

CHECKING THE BODYWORK

Use this diagram to mark any faults, damage or corrosion.

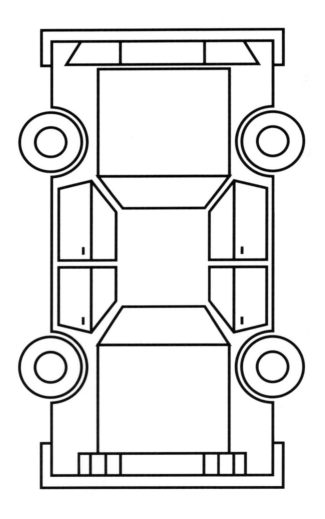

Useful Information

Car inspections

AA	0345 500610
RAC	0800 333660
Automobile Buyers Services	0345 419926
Green Flag	01254 355606

Finding out the car's history

HPI Autodata	01722 422422
AA Car Data Check	0800 234999

Possible problems

If you buy a stolen car, the police can take it from you to return it to the original owner or the insurance company if a claim has been paid. You will not get any compensation, even though you bought the car in good faith. You can sue the seller for your losses, but this might be difficult if you bought privately and the seller has disappeared. If you bought the car on credit, you may still have to pay off the loan; it depends on the type of agreement.

If you buy a car with finance still outstanding, and if the dealer sold the car, the debt is still theirs. Buy privately and you are not liable for the debt, which is 'converted'.

Were you sold a write-off? This is not a criminal offence, provided the car i
not unroadworthy.

If you have a problem with the car, go back to the seller straight away, explai
the problem and say what you want done. It is better to sort out a problem b
mutual agreement, as taking a claim to court is expensive, complicated and ther
is no guarantee that the problem will be resolved. Get the car inspected by
professional and send that report with a solicitor's letter threatening action. Thi
will work with a dealer, but not with an obligation-free private seller.

Were you sold a car with an adjusted mileage? Dealers have to guarantee th
mileage and show evidence that they checked as best they could. A private selle
can't lie, but if they don't guarantee the mileage otherwise, or you don't get ther
to write it on the contract, you have no comeback. Otherwise Trading Standard
(see below) may follow up your claim.

Trading Standards

For complaints about dealers and private sellers you suspect of being dealers
contact your local **Trading Standards Service** (sometimes called the Consume
Protection Department). Their address is in the phone book under your loca
council or, in Northern Ireland, the Department of Economic Development. Or g
to a Citizens Advice Bureau or consumer advice centre. See the phone boo
for details.

   If a dealer is a member, one of the trade associations listed below may be abl
to help. There is a code of practice for dealing with complaints. You can go to cour
or use a trade association conciliation/arbitration scheme.

Other useful organisations

For guidance on where practical help may be obtained if problems arise in th
purchase of goods and services:

Office of Fair Trading Consumer Information Line   0345 22449

For complaints about used cars and repairs/servicing in England, Wales and Northern Ireland:

The National Conciliation Service   0345 585350
Retail Motor Industry Federation (RMIF),
2nd Floor,
Chestnut House,
9 North Street,
Rugby CV21 2AB

For complaints about used cars and repairs/servicing in Scotland:

Customer Complaints Service   0131 225 3643
Scottish Motor Trade Association Ltd,
3 Palmerston Place,
Edinburgh EH12 5AF

For complaints about cars still under a manufacturer's warranty:

The Consumer Relations Adviser Society of Motor Manufacturers & Traders,
Forbes House,
Halkin Street,
London SW1X TDS.

If you are a member of the AA or RAC, they will help if you have problems with buying a used car.

AA   0990 500600
RAC   0990 533533

Index